THE
SOUTHEAST ASIAN CITY

THE
SOUTHEAST ASIAN CITY

A
SOCIAL GEOGRAPHY OF THE PRIMATE CITIES
OF
SOUTHEAST ASIA

★

T. G. McGEE

FREDERICK A. PRAEGER, *Publishers*
New York · Washington

BOOKS THAT MATTER

Published in the United States of America in 1967
by Frederick A. Praeger, Inc., Publishers
111 Fourth Avenue, New York, N.Y. 10003

Second printing, 1969

Copyright © 1967 by G. Bell and Sons, Ltd.

Library of Congress Catalog Card Number: 67-14707

Printed in Great Britain

TO
JOAN

Contents

Tables

8

Figures

9

Plates

Preface

THROUGHOUT THE under-developed world today, the 'primate' cities which dominate the urban centres play a vital role as the main disseminating centres of the social, political and economic innovations which the urban-based governments are attempting to introduce. These cities are the nerve centres from which the sparks of change flow outward in the effort to attain economic development. This study investigates the main features of the growth, characteristics and roles of the great cities in one small sector (the region of Southeast Asia) of this vast segment of the world's humanity, in an attempt to illustrate the broader problems of the cities of the Third World. For this purpose the Southeast Asia region is ideal, for although the cities of the area contain only a small proportion of the urban population of the Third World (20 million out of 334 million), their cultural diversity, their common heritage of colonialism, and their widely varying economic and political systems reinforce the view that the region is a microcosm of the Third World.

There are, of course, problems associated with such an investigation. The title may lead the reader to assume that the writer is attempting to build up some constructed model of the typical Southeast Asian City, after the style of Sjoberg's model of the Pre-industrial City. No such model is attempted for it may be argued with some justification that the economic and political fragmentation of the area which has occurred on an already culturally diversified base inhibits generalization on a regional basis. Nevertheless, it can be argued that there are enough common configurations in the history, economic and social structures and roles of the cities of Southeast Asia to permit some general assessment.

13

Much of the material for this study was collected during a four-year stay at the University of Malaya, which also provided me with a useful base from which to travel to other Southeast Asian countries. The experience and observations carried out during these visits helped me formulate many of the ideas put forward in the text. In addition I have made ample use of the considerable volume of secondary sources on the cities of the region. This material has been further supplemented by government reports and censuses. Where possible I have illustrated the general by case studies drawn from the cities of Southeast Asia with which I am most familiar. Thus Chapters 7, 8 and 9 incorporate some of the urban research which I have carried out in Malaysia and the Philippines. The result is very much in the nature of a preliminary survey, but even in this form it is hoped that it will provoke questions and subsequent research which will broaden our knowledge of the cities of Southeast Asia.

In conclusion I would like to record my thanks to Peter Webster and Ann Magee for a critical reading of the script; to my wife for her brave attempts to make my writing comprehensible; to Mrs. Guerin for typing the script; Mrs. Jean Benfield for photographic assistance; and Mrs. Winchester for drawing the maps. Finally I wish to thank Professors Keith Buchanan and D. W. McKenzie for permission to use several of their photographs.

CHAPTER 1

The Southeast Asian City and the Third World[1]

DURING THE decade of the nineteen-fifties, the world urban population[2] more than doubled, rising from 313 million to 655 million.[3] Even in the earliest period of urban growth which accompanied the industrial revolution in north-western Europe, the world city population did not grow as fast, and while individual cities have experienced similar growth rates, such world-wide increase is unparalleled. The main reason for this urban explosion is the rapid rise in the city populations of the under-developed world. In this vast area, which contains over two-thirds of the world's population, even a very slight increase in urban populations can boost the world's total urban population out of all proportion to the earlier periods of rapid city growth. But in the postwar period the cities of the Third World have grown massively; for instance, the population of Caracas jumped from 350,000 in 1941 to 1½ million in 1963; that of Metropolitan Manila from 1·3 million in 1948 to 2·1 million in 1960, and Greater Bombay from 2·8 million in 1951 to 4·1 million in 1961. Such examples of city growth can be repeated for virtually every Third World country, for their pace is not exceptional. Thus the population growth of the cities of the Third World has contributed almost 200 million of the 342 million world urban population increase in the last decade. These figures are phenomenal when compared with the initial period of the world 'urban revolution' (1800–50) when the city increase in Western Europe was responsible for some 7·3 million of the total world urban population growth of 9·9 million.[4] Yet that 7 million increase in fifty years, a mere 3·5 per cent of the Third World's urban population increase in one decade, represented a far more significant element in the transformation of the societies of that area than does the 200 million increase in one decade in the Third World.

For that 7 million population growth in the urban areas of western Europe was the beginning of the *true urban revolution* which brought about a fundamental change in the structures of the societies of northern Europe, North America and the white-settler colonies of Australia and New Zealand. Beginning in Britain the growing cities gradually absorbed an increasing proportion of the total population until the majority of the total population was living in cities and an 'urbanized society' had come into being.[5] By 1900 Britain was an urbanized society, and other northern European countries, the United States, Canada, Australia and New Zealand soon followed. Basically the reason for the change in the character of human society was simple. The technological innovations which allowed the growth of manufacturing, commerce and services did not rely on land as the main means of production, but used it only as a site, thereby minimizing the friction of space inevitably involved in the division of labour. At the same time as the industrial revolution brought about the increasing concentration of people in the cities, it also introduced the technical improvements which made possible increased productivity in agriculture and allowed the rural population to shift to the cities. Clearly the urbanization process in western Europe and the other capitalist societies was closely related to economic development, and industrialization in particular.

The *true urban revolution* of the industrialized nations transformed rural societies into urban societies, metropolitan countries into countries of megalopoli[6] and gave rise to urbanized societies. The dominant form of human settlement in the industrialized nations is now the city and increasingly the 'giant city'. Giant urban agglomerations now sprawl out, swallowing the countryside, presenting problems of urban congestion, transportation and slums, bringing a whole new way of life into being. The problem of the countryside has been replaced by the problem of the city. What is not so clear is whether the current growth of cities of the Third World is bringing about a transformation in the nature of their societies comparable to that which accompanied the *true urban revolution*. Davis[7] has shown that in the forty under-developed countries for which data is available in the recent decades, the average gain in the proportion of urban population was 20 per cent, compared with an average gain of 15 per cent for sixteen industrialized countries during the decades of their most rapid urbanization. He goes on to argue that despite the present higher rate of urbanization in the under-developed world, the vastly different demographic circumstances of these countries will prevent urbanized societies from coming into being. The prime reason for this situation, he argues, is the fact that natural increase is much higher in the contemporary Third World cities than it was at the same phase of city growth in the industrialized countries. This means it is the 'population boom', not rural-urban migration, which is 'overwhelmingly responsible' for the current growth of cities. This view seems to be opposed by the popular conception that the cities of the Third World are growing largely from rural-urban migration. But as Davis shows conclusively, there is good reason to believe that the rural-urban movement in most of the Third World countries, despite its large volume, does little but make up the difference between the rates of natural increase in city and country. The implications of these facts are that city growth in the non-industrial world is becoming 'increasingly unhinged from economic development and hence from rural-urban migration'.[8] The result of the situation may well be grave, for with few exceptions (Argentine, Japan), population pressures will grow increasingly in the rural areas and the cities already growing mightily from natural increase will not be able to absorb even a fraction of the rural exodus. Thus the majority of Third World countries are undergoing a phase of *pseudo urbanization* and it is deceptive to see the current rapid city growth in the area as indicative of economic development.

Other factors besides the unprecedented growth in population in the non-industrial countries have contributed to this present phase of *pseudo urbanization*. The majority of these Third World countries have inherited their economic structure from an era of colonialism characterized by an excessive specialization in the production of materials for the industries of the metropolitan powers. Despite independence, the economy of the Third World countries is still closely linked and dangerously dependent upon the industrial powers, and this has been one of the factors preventing the widespread industrial development which is necessary if the cities of the Third World are to provide greater employment opportunities for their populations. Despite the enormous advantages of twentieth-century developments in technology, improved transportation and communications, the countries of the Third World have to enter a world market which is beyond their ability to control because of its domination by the industrial nations.[9] The city of the Third World thus retains its economic function as a 'link' between the industrialized powers and the sources of raw materials—a 'transplant' with closer economic ties to the urbanized societies of the industrial world than to the countryside of the Third World.

The failure to industrialize restricts the employment opportunities in the cities and results in both unemployment and under-employment. The number of available jobs has to be considerably in excess of the number needed for efficient management if a large segment of the city population is not going to starve. Thus the tertiary sector of the city's occupational structure grows greatly in excess of what is required. The employed work longer hours for a lower return and the city becomes characterized by the 'shared poverty' pattern.[10] Hawkers, vendors, trishaw drivers, shop assistants, and government employees proliferate in the cities of the Third World. Despite the fact that the city cannot offer employment opportunities, the population still grows from natural increase and rural-urban migration, and the poverty of the majority of the city's population grows greater. The failure to reform the agricultural structures of the majority of the Third World countries means that rural poverty is in no way lessened. This situation together with the pressure of a growing population, forces more migrants into the already overcrowded cities. Cities grow, despite their failure to industrialize, not because of industrialization, as they did in the Western countries.

The significant role that the cities of the Third World play as the main centres of the social and political change which the political *élites* of the new nations are attempting to bring about in their countries, also attracts people to the cities. The majority of the countries of the Third World are passing through a phase of strident nationalism, propagated by the city-based political *élites* in order to build up the loyalty of their populations. It is essentially the emerging middle classes of the cities who are responsible for this growth of nationalism, for not only does '. . . it provide this class with a powerful and believable social rationale for change',[11] it also reinforces the social and political systems which strengthen their power in the country. It is understandable that such groups should seek to transform their societies through Western ideologies and values. Many of the leaders of these nationalistic movements have grown up and been educated in the colonial cities and in various degrees have adopted Westernized patterns of life and thought of their former colonial rulers.[12] The nationalism of the Third World countries, then, is essentially a city-based phenomenon. The city becomes the focus of the educational institutions which train the cadres of the new nationalism; the focus of the political institutions set up to govern the country, and the centre of political, cultural and social life. But the concentration of the new nations' political energies in the cities is not without dangers, for governments become increasingly reliant on small urban middle classes, the industrialists, and merchants—while their failure to solve the wider economic problems of their country alienates the rural population. As de Briey argues, 'It follows therefore that the legitimacy of their claim to power remains in doubt. Unsure of their hold over the masses and being unable to count on the effective and stable support of the rural population, the rulers are tempted to solve their problems in an authoritarian way with the help of their party or the army.'[13] In some ways the cities of the Third World begin to assume the character of the 'cult centres' associated with the pre-industrial era. Only now the rites of nationalism replace the rites of the 'god-king'.

The rapid growth of the Third World cities is evident every-where in their physical appearance. The cities have been growing so fast that the new nations have been unable to provide adequate housing, and city populations are forced into squatter settlements of flimsy miserable huts constructed of makeshift materials which occupy any vacant land in the interstices or fringes of the city. Such areas contrast sharply with the suburbs of the new *élites* with their luxurious houses, new roads and new cars. This juxtaposition of affluence and poverty is one of the most striking features of these cities. The rapid growth of population has also placed tremendous pressure on the available city services. City government, welfare and transportation break down under the explosion of city population. The attempt to build up community and civic pride breaks down under the impact of population growth and 'shared poverty' into a condition of urban anarchy. The end-product is that the cities of the Third World become wastelands, conglomerations of millions of individuals described by Claude Lévi-Strauss,

> . . . Filth, promiscuity, disorder, physical contact; ruins, shacks, excrement, mud; body moistures, animal droppings, urine, purulence, secretions, suppuration—everything that urban life is organized to defend us against, everything we loathe, everything we protect ourselves against at great cost—all these by-products of cohabitation never here impose a limit on its spread. On the contrary, they constitute the natural setting which the town must have if it is to thrive.[14]

The consequences of this period of *pseudo urbanization*, if the earlier analysis is correct, suggest that the results may well be disastrous for the political and social stability of the majority of the Third World countries. But it must be accepted that these conclusions accept a basic underlying premise; namely, that the economic development of the Third World countries involves a shift from rural to urban life and in fact the creation of urbanized societies. It may well be, as Hoselitz points out, that the greater densities of Third World rural populations, particularly in the Asian countries, create the need for such a phenomenal expansion in non-agricultural employment opportunities if the rural population is to be absorbed in the city

sector, that given the present conditions, the necessary central-
ized industrialization could not be achieved.[15] Therefore it
would seem that the agricultural populations of the Third
World countries must in many cases remain a high proportion
of the total population, and some system of decentralized
industry introduced to make use of the surplus rural labour.
This might not necessarily involve a massive shift in population.
In this respect the present developments in China are of
considerable importance to other Third World countries.[16]
But for the moment the city-based political élites of the majority
of the Third World countries seem to be trapped in a descending
spiral of their own making. The cities in which they live
appear to offer the hopes for the future. They are the centres
of innovation, the centres of intellectual activity, political and
administrative control, and the centres of the mobilization of a
labour force which is committed to industry. The future of
their countries is mirrored in the seeming affluence of the city.
It is not surprising that the cities of the Third World assume
such a pre-eminent role in the thinking of the governmental
élites of the Third World.

Meanwhile the vast majority of the population (over 70 per
cent in most cases) remains in the rural sector which
increasingly stagnates under the effects of rapid population
growth and its lack of agricultural reform and increased
agricultural production. More and more of the food production of the countryside is consumed and the towns must look
overseas for food which becomes an important part of the
country's imports; consequently the country's overseas finances
which might have aided economic development, are depleted.
Of course, the Third World cities may be kept going by massive
injections of foreign aid and food as is occurring in Saigon and
the cities of India, but the cities still undergo economic inflation
which further increases their economic problems. It seems that
the growing disparity in development between the town and
country will eventually bring about a situation in which the
poverty of the great mass of the rural population will enforce a
radical solution on these societies. Today the cities of the Third
World are cities of 'hope', for their populations still believe
that their countries will achieve the economic breakthrough

and give them economic equality with the industrialized nations of the world. But much of the evidence suggests that unless rational economic development fostering urbanization and industrialization concurrent with improvements in the agricultural sector (such as has occurred in some of the socialist countries and Japan), the cities of 'hope' will becomes cities of despair. It is a small step from despair to desperation.

The validity of this broad picture of the *pseudo urbanization* of the Third World can only be established through the investigation of the features of urban growth and characteristics of cities in specific countries and regions of the Third World. For such an investigation the Southeast Asian region is ideal, for while the cities contain only a small proportion of the urban population of the Third World (20 million out of 334 million) and thus can hardly be regarded as representative, the rich variety of cities, and the varying forms of political and economic adaptation which are developing in the area ranging from the socialist society of North Vietnam to the capitalist society of the Philippines, have all the complexity of the cities and countries of the Third World.[17]

In common with many other Third World countries, Southeast Asia has a very long and rich history of urban life. Indigenous urban areas have existed since as early as the first century A.D. These cities have performed a large number of functions, acting as political, religious and ceremonial centres as well as important marketing and entrepôt centres for the indigenous Asian trade. They were not superseded in number or importance until the nineteenth century when the extension of Western political control led to the incorporation of the area into the Western-dominated world trade and the establishment of the colonial ports on sea coasts and river estuaries. These ports were the foci of colonial control and domination. They were also administrative, processing and transportation foci, but it was largely their economic function as the focal point for the collection of raw materials and the distribution of imports and exports which led to their massive growth and dominance in the urban hierarchy which persists until today.

The countries of Southeast Asia also share a common

colonial heritage of economic fragmentation, reflected in the varying economic levels and systems of urban places. Thus the mainland states of Burma and Indochina, which were developed as 'rice-bowl' food suppliers of the tropical colonial countries, are characterized by much lower levels of economic development than the other territories and consequently, lower levels of urbanization. In island Southeast Asia the particular form of colonial development emphasized mineral exploitation and the production of crops for the metropolitan powers. Consequently many more towns were established and the levels of urbanization were higher. But throughout Southeast Asia, despite the varying levels of urbanization, the dual urban structure divided between one great city—a Singapore, Rangoon or Manila—and a mass of smaller towns has persisted as one major feature of the urban structure. Finally the cities of most Southeast Asian countries still perform significant roles as the centres of political and social change in which the small political *élites* are struggling with the problems of economic development and building stable nation states.

Despite these obvious similarities with the urban structures of other countries in the non-industrialized world, there are certain unique elements which characterize the pattern of urbanization in Southeast Asia. Surprisingly, Southeast Asia is one of the least urbanized areas in the Third World. In 1960, only 9·1 per cent of its population lived in centres of over 100,000.[18] Of the great regional blocs of the Third World only Africa and perhaps China have a lower level of urbanization. Not only is Southeast Asia one of the least urbanized of the Third World regions, but it also has one of the highest proportions of urban populations concentrated in these large cities. Thus of the urban population resident in centres of over 20,000 the percentage who are concentrated in the large cities exceeding 100,000 is 70 per cent in Thailand, 73 per cent in the Philippines and over 60 per cent in Malaya and Singapore. It is thus not surprising that it is the 'great cities' which dominate the urban structure of Southeast Asia. In Burma, Thailand, Cambodia, South Vietnam and the Philippines the largest urban concentration is at least five times as large as its nearest rival. In Malaysia and Indonesia the dominance of the 'great city' is not nearly as marked, because of the higher levels of economic development in the latter, and the sheer size and regional diversity of Indonesia. Nevertheless, the dominance of the 'primate city' is unquestionably the most important feature of urban structure. So much so that the characteristics of the 'great cities' of Djakarta, Singapore, Rangoon, Bangkok, Manila and Saigon-Cholon are justifiably held to be representative of the characteristics of the pattern of Southeast Asian urbanization for such a considerable proportion of the areas' urban population is resident in them.

All these cities, with the exception of Bangkok, were established by the colonial powers on sites which had assumed little importance in the indigenous era. They grew largely because of their functions as centres of trade, commerce, transport and administration, and they have, as Fisher[19] remarks, retained 'a position of unchallenged supremacy' to the present day. These cities are among the most cosmopolitan in the world. Within their boundaries live some of the most heterogeneous racial populations of any urban areas; Chinese, Indians and the mixed tribal elements of the indigenous populations are economically, residentially and culturally segregated in what have been labelled 'plural societies'. While the life of the city is carried on with a tacit mutual understanding of the various communities enabling them to co-exist peacefully enough, there are always latent tensions underneath. Sometimes these tensions between the races inhabiting the city flare to the surface and erupt in vicious racial, religious or political riots. Tinker cites such an occurrence in pre-war Burma where '. . . in the centre of Rangoon, from three hundred to five hundred Indians were killed and about one thousand injured by Burmese mobs enraged because Indian coolies secured employment before Burmese in the Rangoon docks';[20] more recently there have been similar racial riots in Singapore and Djakarta. But most of the time these tensions remain under the surface; the city mob—the betcha drivers, the 'djembel-djembel' (vagabonds) of Djakarta, the hoodlums, the erratically employed labourers, and the unemployed are too concerned with the suffering of their everyday search for food and employment. The Southeast Asian city is a mosaic of cultural and racial worlds each invoking the memory of other lands and people; the tree-lined avenues of Phnom-Penh and Saigon reminiscent of Paris; the canals and stuffy buildings of old Batavia, replicas of the medieval Dutch town; and the towering skyscrapers of downtown Singapore are part of the universal Western central business district. The bustling overcrowded Chinatowns with their pavements full of hawkers and stalls that reach back into the cool of the open shops; and above the crowded tenements with washing hanging from the open windows—innumerable flags hung for the procession of hawkers, human carriers and grubby children who move along the pavements. The streets of Indian textile sellers—white-draped figures beckoning the potential purchaser with the frenzy of a Greek chorus at the moment of tragedy; inside, bright-saried matronly figures fingering cloth, carrying it to the doorway to see the gold edging of the saris flash in the bright tropical sun; near-by the loan houses of the Chettyar money-lenders sitting cross-legged on long wooden benches, their fingers flicking through account books. The aroma of Indian curries labels the street. The rural quiet sets apart the Malay urban kampong or the Burmese 'kwetthit' where gardens and fruit trees mask the houses and absorb the noise of the Malay or Burmese orchestras from the Japanese transistor radios. Only the cupola of the white mosque or the glinting gold stupa of the Buddhist temple shows above the sea of green tree-tops. Around the city spread the spacious residences of the wealthy *élites* and the less sizeable Western bungalows of the emerging middle class, interspersed with enclaves of attap huts of the poor and dispossessed of the city—the squatters. Here the contrasts are not those of the cultural diversity of the racial worlds of the inner city, but the contrasts of wealth and squalor.

While these 'primate cities' still dominate the urban structure of Southeast Asia, their position has begun to be challenged with the splitting up of the old colonial empires and the formation of new political alignments since the era of independence. Thus, for instance, the former importance of Saigon-Cholon as the commercial centre of French Indochina has been reduced by the independent policies of Cambodia and North Vietnam. Already Phnom-Penh has grown rapidly as the capital of an independent nation, and the Cambodian government has established a new port town of Sihanoukville which replaces Saigon-Cholon as its major port. A similar pattern has occurred in Malaya where Kuala Lumpur has been growing rapidly as the capital of the new nation and an attempt has been made to develop near-by Port Swettenham, in order to reduce the reliance on Singapore. Within other Southeast Asian countries the attempt to develop regions largely ignored during the colonial period has led to the growth of some regional centres. The increasing importance of some urban centres on the island of Mindanao since the Second World War can be cited as one illustration of this trend.[21]

Yet another factor bringing about the growth of new urban centres in Southeast Asia is the geopolitical nature of the area; a region of fragmented and politically weak states which the major antagonists of the Cold War feel outside forces will impinge upon to shape events. Thus the Americans and their allies have created a series of military, naval and air-bases in the area which form a ring of urban bastions adding a new element to the urban network in Thailand, Malaya and the Philippines. The best example of this process at present in operation can be seen in South Vietnam where the Americans are constructing a completely new set of ports, military and air centres throughout the country. These are not simply foreign bases which will disappear in time, because the possibilities of employment they provide for the local population and the needs of the military personnel attracts a substantial population to the vicinity of the base, thus bringing about permanent settlement. This point is well illustrated by Olongopo, a shanty town of 80,000 people located outside the U.S. Navy's main base for the Seventh Fleet—Subic Bay in the Philippines. Here the majority of the indigenous population earn their living from the base. Some are employed as technicians and labourers within the base itself, but the majority earn their income in the 300 nightclubs, restaurants, shops and cocktail lounges that provide entertainment for the sailors. It has been estimated that sailors on leave often spend as much as $23 million a year in the town, providing its main source of revenue. Thus the period of political, economic and social change since the Second World War is bringing about new urban patterns in Southeast Asia.

While the features of the Southeast Asian cities do show considerable diversity and variance from other Third World cities, there can be little question that they share the same problems of rapid city growth experienced by other cities of the Third World; the economic problems of unemployment, unbalanced occupational structures, poverty and inequality of incomes; the social problems of the in-migrant and the problems of adjustment to city life which so often lead to delinquency and crime; the physical problems of overcrowding in tenement slums and burgeoning squatter settlements, and the administrative problems of establishing efficient urban services in the face of this urban explosion. These problems overwhelm the administrators of the Southeast Asian city and force them to adopt temporary measures rather than long-range comprehensive schemes.

It is not uncommon for writers to portray the Southeast Asian city as a centre of social, political and economic change and to suggest that the changes are illustrative of wider changes occurring throughout the society. While it cannot be denied that the cities with their growing middle class, their aggressive modernism and signs of Westernization appear to be changing, it is dangerous to suggest that this change is mirrored in the wider society. It may even be questioned whether the visual evidence of progress in the great cities of Southeast Asia—the new buildings, the new monuments and wide roads—does not in fact mask widespread poverty and lack of social change. As one writer comments, 'Put in another way, the luxuriant tropical vegetation in the rural areas, like the new buildings in the towns, conceals poverty and shades the fact that the urban-rural, rich-poor gaps are widening.'[22] It has always been customary to regard the city as the centre of innovation and change, in contrast to the countryside which is traditional and unchanging, a viewpoint which is supported by the actions of the present urban-centred governments of the majority of Southeast Asian countries. But it must not be forgotten that the majority of Southeast Asia's people are still peasants and it is only by fundamental changes in the countryside that the great advances necessary in economic and social development can be made. It is necessary to understand not only the character of the present-day cities of Southeast Asia but also the relationship of the city-based *élites* and the rural peasantry. It is also necessary to understand and analyse the attempts or the political *élites* to change the attitudes of the rural population with the aid of the contemporary communications revolution and the slogans of nationalism.

Above all it is fundamental to understand the economic relationships between the city and countryside, for these two regional sectors are inextricably linked. While it may be possible for economic plans to proceed for some time without acknowledging this fact; for instance, some writers have argued that the necessary capital for industrialization in the cities can be raised through the taxation of the rural sector, eventually the social and political consequences of such policies will be the alienation of the rural populations from the city-based govern-ments. The result will be political instability and the slowing down of economic growth. Whatever the economic rationale, it is clear that the future of the Southeast Asian countries rests largely on the ability of the present governments to prevent social and political antagonisms between the city and country-side emerging.

CHAPTER 2

The Indigenous Cities of Southeast Asia: The Phase of Primary Urbanization

THE ORIGINS of urban settlement in Southeast Asia are obscure. Most historical evidence indicates that the earliest cities originated as a result of the diffusion into the area of Chinese and Indian forms of political organization and religion from the first century A.D. Prior to this date, political power was scattered throughout the area in a series of tribal cells. These tribal societies existed in a delicate ecological balance with the physical environment because of their limited technology, which forced them to move frequently in search of food and prevented the development of a stable relationship with the environment as well as occupational specialization emerging.[1] But the considerable growth of trading contacts with the area from the first century onwards, together with the actual extension of Chinese control into North and Middle Vietnam, brought the tribal chiefs into contact with the systems of belief and political organizations of these 'high civilizations', particularly those systems associated with Indian civilization.[2] The actual manner in which these first cities grew up has not been documented, but it would appear that the growth of trading ports associated with the adoption by the tribal chiefs of Indian forms of political organization, based on Brahmanic and Buddhist beliefs provided the combination of economic, political and social forces which brought the first cities into being.

Just what importance in early city formation can be attached to these various economic, political, technological and social forces is impossible to determine. Certainly the adoption of the concept of 'deva-raja'[3] by many of the tribal chiefs enabled

29

them to become the '. . . visible manifestations of the god-head',[4] and provided the cosmological justification for the growth of specialized groups of retainers who carried on the ritualistic functions associated with kingship, as well as the necessity for the creation of the symbols of 'divineness'—the palace, the throne, the tiered umbrella, the lingam—all enclosed within the walls of the 'sacred city'.[5] In addition there must have been economic and technological develop-ments in agriculture and transportation which allowed this non-productive group of specialists to be fed. At least in the beginning the majority of these cities must have been small centres relying on a combination of trade and small agricultural surpluses to ensure their existence. It was only after five centuries that the political, economic and technological developments led to a division of functions between the two main types of early urban centres—the sacred city and the market city. In the sacred city, 'the supreme symbol of the state within the unifying cosmology which links together earth and heaven',[6] the wealth was gained from appropriating agricultural surpluses and labour from the rural hinterland; and in the market cities, the wealth came from the royal authorities' use of maritime power to ensure their control of trade, or their granting of privileges to foreigners to use their city as a trading port.

It is true that some historians have cast doubts as to whether cities ever existed, arguing that these early centres were 'cult centres' where the agricultural surpluses were regarded as a tribute, for the support of a non-productive *élite* class, uncon-cerned with the economic development of the country. Thus Coe has argued that,

> A surplus is surely the precondition of civilization, for lacking it a society cannot support the non-food producing specialists (like priests and artisans) who are the creators of civilization. As already mentioned, what matters is what becomes of this surplus. In the urban organic civilizations it is consumed by the cities; in the non-urban unilateral civilizations it is taken as a tribute for the support of cult centres.[7]

What Coe seems to ignore is that even in a Southeast Asian

centre such as Angkor, there is considerable evidence of trade and diversification of economic activity which supports the argument that such centres deserve the title of city. Whatever the arguments for or against the existence of early urban settlements, it is hard not to agree with Spencer's summary of the functions of the city, even if it did not rest on the same economic basis as the modern Western city,

> The city was the chief consumer of agricultural surpluses, the point of accumulation of wealth and tradition, and the chief developer of cultural patterns—the centre of civilization. It was the nerve centre of the state and the chief object of attack by an invader.[8]

The first urban settlements that grew up in Southeast Asia were clearly associated with foreign trading contacts although the process did involve a considerable amount of adaptation to incorporate elements of the indigenous cultures. Historical evidence suggests that there were three main areas of urban settlement established by the end of the second century A.D. These were the empires of Funan located in the region of the lower Mekong and its delta, the Champa empire, situated in the neighbourhood of modern Hué, and the empire of Langkasuka, located on the Kra Isthmus, from which it could control over-land ties with the opposite side of the Malay peninsula. While the economic base of the capital cities of these empires is not clearly established, they gained some wealth from their position on the trade route between China and India. Vyadhapura, the capital of the Funan Empire, located some twenty miles from the coast, on which was sited Oc Eo, its port, was an early centre of foreign merchants. Descriptions of the city rely largely on a third-century Chinese account which describes the ruler as claiming descent from an Indian Brahmin prince bearing the imperial title of 'king of the Mountain', and the people as practising a primitive kind of agriculture:[9] indirect evidence at least of the assertion that the city relied largely on trade for its wealth. With such a small agricultural base, it must have been difficult for the king to have appropriated the labour necessary to build the stone temples and other symbols of his royalty. Perhaps this is why there are no archaeological remains of Vyadhapura comparable to Angkor Thom.

These city states proliferated throughout mainland Southeast Asia in this early period. Notable amongst them was Nakorn Pat'om (probably built as a coastal port but today thirteen miles inland), which was the centre of the powerful state of Dvaravati in the valley of the Chao Phraya in Thailand. Similar states also grew up in the Malayan archipelago where a fragmented physical environment did not provide a favourable land base for the extensive control of agriculture by the king. There was only one exception to this—the area of East Central Java where the fertile volcanic soil and plentiful water provided a favourable milieu for the development of irrigation and 'agrarian-based' sacred cities. The most important of the early trade-based empires was the Sumatran state of Srivijaya, on the Palembang River, which reached the peak of its power by the eighth century. The capital itself was described as a city built on rafts along the edge of the river, with a sparsely populated and poorly cultivated hinterland. Srivijaya drew its economic wealth from its role as an important entrepôt port and trading emporium. Other centres of power which grew up contemporaneously with the control of archipelago seas by Srivijaya were the agrarian-based Sailendra dynasty in Java during the eighth century, and in the ninth century the Khmer Empire based on the city complex of Angkor. During the same period, the Burmese were colonizing Upper Burma and by the eleventh century their great capital of Pagan was established.

The full sequence of dates and names of the various states is not necessary to provide a background for investigating the more general characteristics of the various pre-industrial cities which were the 'nerve centres' of these empires. The broad division between 'sacred cities' and 'market cities' already suggested is a useful enough division for the analysis of the broad range of pre-industrial cities that grow up in Southeast Asia. The 'market cities' have generally preceded the land-based cities in Southeast Asia, growing up from the first century, both in mainland Southeast Asia and insular Southeast Asia. Such cities drew their economic wealth from maritime trade and their role as trading emporiums. The population of such cities was cosmopolitan and fluctuated sharply in size in response to the city states' control of trade. The social structure of these maritime city states was characterized by the abrupt division between the king, his courtiers, and the rest of the population, and found its physical evidence in the morphology of the city, with its sharply demarcated foreign quarters. However, the influence of the merchant, the peddler, and the remainder of the commercial groups was much stronger than in the land-based cities. Frequently the palace *élite* indulged in commerce of various kinds. These 'market cities' have persisted throughout the history of city growth in Southeast Asia, sometimes coexisting within the same realm as land-based cities as, for instance, in Java.[10]

The sacred cities drew their economic wealth from the great agrarian civilizations of Southeast Asia. They were administrative, military and cultural centres of empires that drew their power from the tribute of conquered territories, and the labour supplies which could be manipulated by the rulers. This is not to say that trade was not important in such cities; substantial trade was indeed carried on in such empires as that of the Khmers; but it was not the major source of wealth and power. The peak of the agrarian-based cities was almost certainly reached during the second half of the first millennium when the greatest outburst of city building occurred prior to the considerable growth of cities in the nineteenth century.

The differences in the economic base, the limitations of topography, and the varying capacities of the early rulers to build their cosmological beliefs into the reality of a city led to considerable differences between the various cities of Southeast Asia. But the most marked differences in morphology occurred between the maritime-based market towns and the agrarian-based 'sacred cities'. Spencer has commented upon the transient character of the former, located on sites which were subject to silting and relying for their wealth on the vagaries of maritime trade. Their location on shore-lines or river banks, with only limited hinterlands, often meant there was inadequate space for city expansion and a large proportion of the population lived on boats or on stilted houses built over the water.[11] Thus the sixteenth-century descriptions of Brunei as a city built on the water are still applicable today. Similarly, Srivijaya's capital was a city of rafts floating on the Palembang River. It is not surprising therefore, that the architectural remnants of these cities are small and scattered, for not only were they built largely of wood, but the kings were unable to appropriate the labour to build the stone monuments of the sacred cities. If present-day Brunei township is at all typical, these cities must have had an essentially transient and temporary appearance. This is not to deny that the cities did not show signs of planning. The careful demarcation of areas for the various foreign trading groups and the location of the palace and the market place in the coastal cities of Java is at least one example of the planning of the trade-orientated cities of the coast.

Compared to the 'sacred cities', however, the coastal cities must have had a chaotic appearance, for whereas the coastal city's often suffered from the fluctuations of trade, the sacred city's plan was a reflection of the cosmological beliefs of the ruler, and therefore had to be adhered to if possible. Tinker has assigned the origins of these systems of belief which were responsible for these heavenly cities. '. . . to Sumeria, and the Ziggurat or Mountain of God which was erected by successive Sumerian rulers. These Ziggurats were temples, with successive levels of terraces which were artificial reproductions of the planes of the universe. The system spread to northwestern India, to the Chou and Han kingdoms, and to Southeast Asia, where it survives until the present day'.[12] Thus the capital city in which the 'god-king' lived was a sacred city, the 'meeting point of heaven, earth and hell',[13] and its location was selected only after careful application of the geomantric art. Because it was a sacred city it was almost invariably planned and constructed as an image (of the universe) of the cosmological beliefs of the society. The main elements of the city, the principal temples, the king's palace, the city walls and moats were located in a manner designed to reproduce the cosmological heaven. Thus cities such as Pagan, and Angkor were carefully planned, and while certain variations did occur in the plans of the cities, due to the varying topography of the sites in which they were located, and the need for defence, these inland cities do have remarkable similarities in their city plans.

The palace and the principal temples could generally be found in the centre of the city, and about them were located the residences of the city *élite* and functionaries. Surrounding this area were streets of artisans, manufacturers, jewellers and

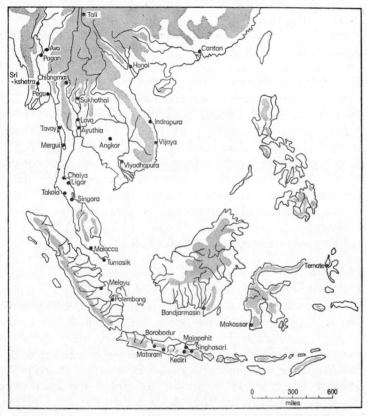

1 The location of the main pre-industrial cities in Southeast Asia, *c.* A.D. 750–1400. The shaded areas are above 500 feet in height.

armourers. The communities of foreign merchants were located outside the city walls, together with the poorer elements of the population. The distribution of power and the social structure were reflected in the grading of social prestige from

35

the centre to the periphery. While such cities were constructed for more permanence than the coastal cities, their stability depended largely on the prestige and power of the king. Thus an entire city could be relocated at the whim of a king—an event which occurred as recently as 1857 when the king of the Upper Burmese Kingdom shifted his capital from Ava Amarapura and founded the city of Mandalay, the last of the great pre-industrial cities.[14] The association of the charisma and power of the king with his city cannot be emphasized too much for the collapse and decline of the city upon the death and defeat of a king is a recurrent feature of the great pre-industrial cities of Southeast Asia.

It is tempting to try to give this distinction between the two types of city some regional meaning by suggesting that the sacred cities were located primarily in mainland Southeast Asia; the market cities in insular Southeast Asia. But a cursory glance at Figure 1 reveals that no such neat pattern existed, the two types of city sometimes coexisted as in Java. The broad discussion of the features of the pre-industrial cities of Southeast Asia can be illustrated in more detail by reference to two cities—Angkor Thom 'The City of Gods', and Malacca, 'A City that was made for Merchandise'.

ANGKOR THOM—'The City of Gods'

The city of Angkor Thom built in the reign of Jayavarman VII, represents the final peak of city and temple building in the Khmer Empire, which had begun with the founding of the Angkor Kingdom by Jayavarman II in A.D. 802. Indravarman who reigned over the Khmer Empire from A.D. 877 to 890 established the real power of Angkor by creating an irrigation complex which made it possible to exploit the land more efficiently and to utilize the labour supply for city building. Reviving the old captive water technique of ancient Chen-La, he built an artificial lake, some 4,000 yards long by 850 yards wide, (The Western Baray) which held the waters of two rivers. The lake was built up on a higher level than the surrounding rice fields, thus allowing water to flow from the baray to irrigation channels in the fields. Later rulers extended and improved this irrigation system providing the high level of agricultural technology which allowed the city of Angkor Thom to exist. The city of Angkor Thom was built in a little over forty years, between A.D. 1181 and 1219. While certain necessities of defence conditioned the plan of the city, the basic city plan was a reflection of agro-religious factors. As Coedès has commented, 'Unlike our western cities, it was not just a group of houses, a market and a seat of government. It was a replica in miniature of the fabled world of Hindu cosmology, a small model of the universe, a microcosm.'[15]

While Hindu and Buddhist doctrines differ in some parts of their cosmology, they both have as central to their beliefs the idea of a magical mountain which is the axis of the universe. On its summit dwell the gods whom they worship, and surrounding the mountain area spread a series of lower continents and oceans where men and spirits live. Angkor Thom is an attempt to recreate this cosmological belief pattern in the form of a city. As one writer has said, '. . . in studying the archaeological map of the Angkor region, we are seeing only the religious skeleton of a city'[16] (see Figure 2). At the centre of the city was the Bayon, the largest temple, a huge mountain in stone—the abode of the gods. Surrounding the Bayon there was an enclosure in which the palace of the king was located and surrounding this were the walls and a wide moat, some eight miles in circumference, which represented the mountain, walls, and the sea of the cosmological universe. The walls and moats also performed an important function of defence. The moat was crossed by five stone causeways leading up to five gates, and there were numerous other temples beyond the enclosure of Angkor Thom.

The population of Angkor Thom must have been considerable. Briggs comments, that 'It was more spacious than any of the medieval walled cities of Europe and could easily have contained the Rome of Nero's day.'[17] It is likely, too, that the enclosure of Angkor Thom, the area within the moat, was essentially the royal city—a religious, administrative and aristocratic centre where the king, the priesthood, the army, the civil functionaries, the main artisans and merchants lived. The surrounding area was made up of a combination of densely-packed villages separated by rice fields and vegetable plots,

palms and fruit trees. Canals from the Baray ran through the
city, irrigating the land and providing the principal means of
transport for the population.

The city gained much of its wealth from the contribution of
the surrounding population. This appears to have been done
through the paying of tributes to specific temples within the

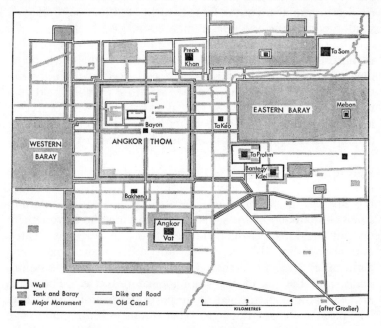

2   Plan of the Angkor city complex, c. A.D. 1200.

city. Some idea of the population engaged in servicing one
temple (not the major temple complex of Angkor Thom), can
be gauged from the fact that the temple of Ta Prohm owned
3,140 villages requiring the service of '. . . 79,365 people, of
whom 18 were great priests; 2,740 officiates, 2,202 assistants,
and 615 dancers'.[18]   At its peak, it is estimated that the whole
city required the services of over '306,000 persons in 13,500
villages devoted to the support of the Khmer temples and their
cults'.[19]   The administration of the Angkor Empire which
collected this tribute and controlled the surrounding areas was

complex. The whole of the country was divided into village communities, each of which paid tribute to the city. There were systems of social welfare and hospitals established by the rulers which extended throughout the territories of the Khmer Empire. Trade flourished, for Chinese sources tell of Indian and Chinese commerce by which rice, spices, cardamons were brought from Angkor, other important produce coming to Angkor from other countries.

Angkor Thom, then, was no small temple carved out of the jungle, but a thriving city representing the culmination of a great series of empires and a complex pattern of cosmological beliefs. The reasons for the decline of the empire from the thirteenth century onwards are complex. While the military invasions of the Siamese brought about the eventual collapse, Coedes argues that this could not have occurred if the people had not been brought to a point of exhaustion by the megalomaniacal building programmes of Jayavarman VII. In addition there seems to have been a decline in the irrigation systems and a consequent decrease in production which also hurried the collapse. Finally Coedès quotes with approval Finot's argument that the religion of the Siamese conquerors must also have had considerable appeal to the Khmer population.

> The religion so aptly described by Louis Finot who knew it well, was Buddhism of the Lesser Vehicle, imported from Ceylon to Siam through the Mons and the Burmans. Basically opposed to individual personality, this Buddhism without deities, so different from that of Jayavarman VII, could not but destroy the cult which was both personal and nationalistic, and which forced the people to worship the god-king and the deified princes.[20]

The parallel between the Angkor of Jayavarman and the modern capitals of Southeast Asia is only too apparent.

MALACCA—'A City that was made for Merchandise'[21]

The city of Malacca showed many sharp contrasts to Angkor Thom. Located on a coastal site which, in its initial stages, provided a defensible hill site from which to control the narrow straits between Sumatra and the Malayan Peninsula—a supremacy which was enforced by a fleet of boats which forced boats calling at Malacca to pay taxes and levies. Malacca, established some time during the fourteenth century, had control over much of Malaya and the East Coast of Sumatra by the end of the fifteenth century.

The economic base of Malacca was first and foremost trade. Unlike many of the ports of Sumatra, such as Tamali, Malacca did not rely upon its hinterland for its wealth. 'The life blood of Malacca was commerce.'[22] Its location at a point where the staple produce of the region passed through a narrow channel, together with the favourable seasonal patterns of wind, meant that Malacca became the collecting centre for the produce (mainly spices) of the archipelago and a distributing point for the Indian textiles.

It was natural that in such a city the population, unlike Angkor Thom, would be ethnically diverse. Traders from the Sumatran ports across the straits, Bengalese, Gujaratis, Tamils and Arabs thronged the city, making it a cosmopolitan and heterogeneous city. Nevertheless, it was a Malay Sultanate ruled by a Malay *élite* who from the middle of the fifteenth century adopted the Islamic religion. The internal pattern of the city, during the period of the Malacca Sultanate, gives some idea of the social structure and the patterns of administration. St. Paul's Hill was maintained as a walled-off precinct in which were located the Sultan's palace and his retinue. The chief administrative officer was the Bendahara who was responsible for administering taxes, the conduct of military campaigns, and the general administration of the city. The homes of the immigrant Malays were located around the slopes of St. Paul's Hill and on the far side of the Malacca Estuary, while the community of Orang Laut took up a site close to the water's edge. Down by the water was the business quarter of the town with the main bazaar situated on a stone bridge spanning the river. The wealthier merchants lived to the north of the river and maintained business offices in the town (see Figure 3).

The population of Malacca never assumed the proportions of Angkor Thom. In fact it showed considerable seasonal fluctuations rising during the peak trading periods and falling during the off-season. Certainly the population does not seem to have risen above 10,000 at any time prior to its capture by the Portuguese at the beginning of the sixteenth century. By that date Malacca—a cosmopolitan, thriving port under the absolute rule of a prince, who maintained himself and the port through taxes and levies on the goods which were exchanged in the town—represented a vastly different city to the

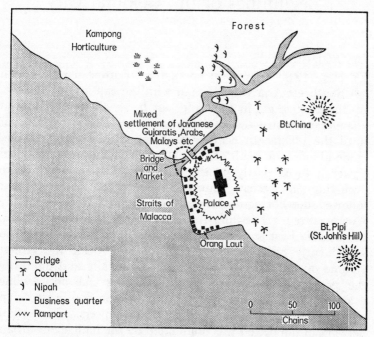

3 Sketch map of the Malay city of Malacca, *c.* A.D. 1500.

'sacred city' of Angkor Thom. It was through such ethnically mixed trade-orientated cities that the first contacts between the West and Southeast Asia occurred; these cities were in many ways the precursors of the colonial cities of the nineteenth century.

CHAPTER 3

The Impact of the West and the Beginnings of the Colonial City

INTRODUCTION

THE FIRST significant contacts of European power with Southeast Asia which began with the capture of Malacca by the Portuguese in 1511 did not bring about pronounced changes in the structure of Southeast Asian society. It was not until the nineteenth century that the truly radical changes came about as a result of the extension of European political power induced partly by the economic changes which were occurring in western Europe. The three centuries that followed the Portuguese capture of Malacca were essentially Asian-centred. The inter-Asian trade in which China, India, the Middle East and the Southeast Asian countries figured so prominently continued and counted for by far the largest volume of the trade in that area.[1] Politically and militarily the power of the Southeast Asian states did not decline dramatically, although the control of certain Southeast Asian seas did pass into the hands of European powers. The urban network of the period was dominated by the indigenous urban centres and, with the exception of the Spanish Philippines and Dutch Java, the European powers did not attempt to establish a fixed urban network within the countries of their interest. Their aims were largely to gain control of the sea routes and the rich indigenous trade of the area. As such they were anxious to establish 'stabilizing points' such as Malacca, Batavia, Manila, and Macao to serve as permanent bases for their forces—entrepôt ports for the goods they collected from the Southeast Asian area, centres of political decision, and most important, places of contact with their more transitory and far-flung garrison and trading contacts in this area.

It should not be imagined that the role played by these early urban settlements was entirely concerned with military and trading functions. The role that urban settlement played in the dissemination of new religions throughout the area is of considerable significance. In the Philippines it was the missionary settlement which was the base from which the Christian faith was propagated. In Indonesia and the Malay Peninsula it was the coastal towns which were the base from which Islam was disseminated to become the main religion.[2] The close relationship between religion and the city has been a fundamental feature of the history of Southeast Asian urbanization.

It is possible to postulate a colonial-urban hierarchy at this period characterized by, first, the stabilized settlements, such as Batavia or Manila; secondly, the garrison and trading settlements, such as Bencoolen, Makassar and Ambon; and thirdly the trading contact points where colonial powers had established trading treaties with indigenous rulers. Here factories or residences of traders associated with the colonial power might be located in the vicinity of the indigenous city as was well illustrated in the case of Ayuthia[3] or Patani. The principal exception to this general colonial-urban pattern is the Philippines where an urban network was a fundamental necessity for Spanish political and religious control. The establishment of Spanish control in this area has sometimes been described as a combination of the power of the cross and sword, but in terms of the establishment of the urban network, the missionaries unquestionably played the major role. It is true that in some cases some of the indigenous settlements such as Cebu and Manila were taken by military conquest, but the majority of urban settlements were established as the result of missionary endeavour. By the end of the eighteenth century, over 1,000 settlements had been founded by the various missionary groups. In the heart of all these towns the missionaries erected a church and convent around the traditional plaza, the heart of the old Spanish town—'Religion was placed at the centre of the city as they meant to place it at the centre of life.'[4]

While the increase in the number and variety of urban settlements between 1500 and 1800 was considerable, the

43

predominant settlement type of Southeast Asia still remained largely that of the closed indigenous village society. The population resident in cities still remained an insignificant proportion of the total population, as it does even today. It is

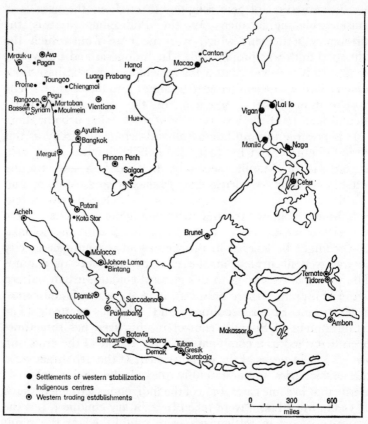

4 The location of the main pre-industrial cities in Southeast Asia, A.D. 1511–1786.

possible to distinguish three main types of urban settlement during this period. First, the agrarian-based indigenous cities, such as Mrauk-u or Ayuthia, which represented a continuation of the great pre-industrial cities of earlier centuries. Secondly, the indigenous commercial centres, largely coastal in location, which in particular proliferated on the northern coast

44

of Java during this period. Thirdly, the centres of colonial power and contact. Their great variety makes the task of grouping them in any set of representative categories exceptionally difficult. It is possible, however, to suggest a rough division between the permanent stabilized centres of colonial power such as Spanish Manila and Dutch Batavia and the garrison fort settlements such as Portuguese Malacca. The remainder of this chapter discusses and illustrates these main types of urban settlement by reference to particular examples (see Figure 4).

THE INDIGENOUS CITY—*Mrauk-u: Capital of Arakan*

In common with the other Southeast Asian mainland states, a series of city states based largely on river locations grew up in Burma from the fourth century onwards. They reached their peak with the Pagan Dynasty of the eleventh century. From its capital at Pagan in the central Burmese lowlands the Empire controlled as far as the westward coast of Burma, including the area of Arakan. In the twelfth and thirteenth centuries, however, Arakan assumed independence from Pagan, and began to emerge as an important maritime state in the Bay of Bengal. An excellent account of the capital of this Arakan empire occurs in Maurice Collis' descriptions of the journey of Manrique (a Portuguese Friar), at the beginning of the seventeenth century.[5] Mrauk-u, the capital of the Arakan Empire, was situated some fifty miles from the coast in the centre of a wide alluvial valley formed by three rivers flowing to the Bay of Bengal. The valley was a wide rice plain which produced more than enough rice for the Empire of Arakan. In fact, rice was exported to India[6] and in return, woods, metals and textiles were imported in ample quantities for the needs of the Mrauk-u city *élites*. Through this wide alluvial plain ran a considerable network of waterways. Collis comments, 'One travelled by them instead of by road; the towns and villages were on or near their banks. It followed that the country was full of boats, from canoes carved from a single tree trunk to substantial cargo boats and vessels capable of carrying many passengers.'[7] The population was concentrated in villages tightly packed on the alluvial plain. There was also a well-developed network of towns. Mrauk-u was the capital, but there were important ports at Akyab and Peroem. In addition, there were numerous Buddhist sites for Arakan was a sacred country, the heart of Buddhism. In fact, Friar Manrique had his first audience with the King of Arakan at the most revered of the sites, the Mahamuni shrine which contained important Buddhist relics, to which the King and his court had travelled in bamboo pavilions built on rafts. The King's bamboo pavilion was a miniature of his palace at Mrauk-u with numerous rooms for his retinue.

In the centre of the city of Mrauk-u was the palace compound forming an inner city. There were three enclosures in the palace compound which rose in tiers, each bounded by a thick stone wall. The circumference of the outermost wall was 2,000 yards, the sides varying from a quarter to one-third of a mile. The palace compound's greatest width did not exceed 620 yards. The main palace buildings were made of teak wood, lacquered and gilded; the roofs were carved with figures and rose in spires. The outer city, which together with the palace city covered an area of twelve square miles, was only partly encompassed by a stone wall. In places, lakes and canals performed defensive functions. Outside the city wall itself was the suburb of Daingri-pet where the Portuguese mercenaries, together with other foreigners employed by the King, resided. Even within the city itself waterways were the principal highways of communication. The houses were built of wood on high wooden posts; their roofs thatched with palm leaves. Plate 11 shows the city's rural appearance.

The political power of the city was vested in the hands of the King and his advisers, but it must be stressed that this power rested on a complex base of religious sanction, for the state was a Buddhist country and the Buddhist monks and astrologers were powerful influences in the city's power structure. The social structure of the city was divided into five groups; the King and his most important advisers, the aristocratic nobles, Buddhist monks and astrologers, the common people, and the foreign mercenaries and traders who resided outside the city wall.

The economic wealth of Mrauk-u was primarily provided by the surplus of rice which not only provided food for the city, but was exported as well. In addition there were large numbers of Indian slaves who provided labour for building projects. The Empire was divided into twelve provinces, each of which was ruled by a governor appointed by the King. Mrauk-u had constant contact with outside empires and people but this did little to change its indigenous character. While the kingdom employed European mercenaries and had contacts with European traders, it remained like many of the mainland indigenous centres of this period, little affected by European contact. European contact, then, remained essentially minor on the mainland of Southeast Asia until the beginning of the nineteenth century.

THE INDIGENOUS COMMERCIAL CENTRE—Bantam: a Javanese harbour principality

While many accounts occur of the Javanese harbour principalities which existed in great profusion during the period of Indonesian trade supremacy in the fourteenth, fifteenth and sixteenth centuries, by far the most detailed are the Dutch accounts of the port of Bantam, situated on the northwest coast of Java, close to present-day Djakarta. It is a pity that more thorough accounts of the towns of northeast Java do not exist because as van Leur points out, 'The centre of Javanese political and maritime power lay after all in such towns as Tuban, Jaratan, Grise, Surabaya, Demak and Japara.'[8] Bantam, originally a port of little significance, was occupied by followers of the Sultan of Demak in 1527, with the overt purpose of using it as a military base to provide strength in the war against the Portuguese who had recently conquered Malacca. Developments in the following century, however, saw the town and its surrounding area break away from the Demak Sultan and become independent. Unlike Mrauk-u, Bantam was a trading port that drew its wealth from the rich spice trade of the Indonesian archipelago. Political power rested in the hands of the ruler and his nobility, and while the ruler and his nobles based much of their power on agrarian possessions, subject villages and slaves, they also drew wealth from their involvement in shipowning and from the taxing of trade goods which came to the city.

47

The major part of the trade, however, was in the hands of what van Leur describes as a 'bourgeois patriciate', some of whom were foreigners. In the case of Bantam they were largely Chinese, because it was the southern port of the Chinese trade. In fact, the chief administrative official for shipping and trade, the Shah Bandar, was a Chinese. Whether the symbolic centre of the city was the market or the Sultan's palace is a debatable point, but there is no doubt that the market, located outside the city gates to the east of the city, was the chief attraction for the numerous and heterogeneous population that peopled the city. Bantam was one of the principal ports of the international Asian trade. Here one found the textiles of India and China, and the jewels of other countries, spread out in the market to be exchanged for the goods of Indonesia, imported particularly from the spice islands.

The city of Bantam was laid out in a series of quarters, each of which was under the control of a noble, and each of whom maintained an armed retinue of warriors, mercenaries and slaves. The only foreign community to live within the city walls were the Chinese, a significant indication of their importance in the trade of the city. The other foreign communities, whether they were Indians, such as the Gujaratis, and even the foreign Indonesians, lived outside the city walls in the suburbs. The social and political structure of the city was divided into two broad groups. The nobles and merchant gentlemen were widely separate from the mass of peddlers, craftsmen, peasants and slaves, but within the first group the nobles had greater political power than the merchant community. The population, augmented as it was by a sizeable number of traders who arrived during the seasons when the markets functioned, fluctuated considerably, but there was throughout a permanent population which was quite sizeable. Trade, the *raison d'être* for the city's existence, was carried on at all social levels. Thus the nobility as well as the peddler were involved in the commercial business of the city. Like any mediaeval city in western Europe there must have been wide variations in the weights and measures as well as in the currency and the manner of bargaining for goods which were used in the market place.

Bantam was a city of trade, orientated towards the international world rather than the local world.

THE EUROPEAN 'TRANSPLANT'—*Malacca and Batavia*

The first European cities which grew up in Southeast Asia were essentially 'transplants' of the European town of the time. The degree to which their morphology and character approximated to the European town depended a great deal on the function of the settlement. Thus garrison towns, such as Portuguese Malacca, utilized the basic morphology of the pre-industrial city, incorporating the European elements only within the fort area. Other settlements which were intended to form permanent settlements for European colonists were laid out as a 'replica' of the mother country's towns. This type of European transplant is well illustrated by the capital of the Dutch in Indonesia—Batavia.

After its capture by the Portuguese in 1511, Malacca underwent few radical changes in its basic city plan.[9] The Portuguese occupied the defensive site of St. Paul's hill, formerly occupied by the Sultan's palace, enclosing their town by a stone wall some twenty feet high and five feet thick. Within the walls the various buildings necessary for the Portuguese administration were constructed, notably the residences of the Governor, the Bishop and other officials, a town hall, a number of churches and two hospitals. Christianity became the major official religion replacing the Muslim practices of the Malay Sultan (see Figure 5).

The various ethnic Kampongs or districts which had existed in the pre-industrial city continued to persist, if anything becoming more clearly demarcated. In the suburb of Upe where the foreign merchants were located, each group had its own quarter: the Indians located in Kampong Kling, the Chinese in Kampong China, and there was an important Javanese quarter as well. Along the river were scattered the houses of Malays, whose occupations were not part of the large-scale commerce of the city, but largely concentrated in fishing, timber cutting and charcoal making.

The imposition of Portuguese rule certainly led to an increase in the city's population for there is evidence that the Portuguese encouraged Chinese immigration and the number of traders who settled permanently in the city increased considerably.[10]   But Portuguese rule did not lead to any radical changes in the social structure of the city.   The Bishop replaced the Imam, the Governor replaced the Sultan and the Portuguese citizen possibly assumed more importance in the

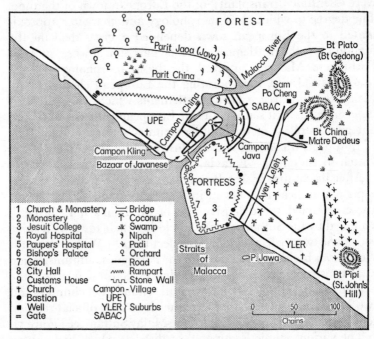

5   Plan of Portuguese Malacca (after Kernial), *c.* 1600.

social structure than his Malay counterpart, but the merchants still retained their importance in the city's society.   Nor did the morphology of the city change dramatically, apart from the addition of the stone buildings and walls of Fort A'Famosa. Portuguese Malacca was essentially a fusion of two cultural variants of this type of pre-industrial settlement.

The founding of Batavia, capital of the Dutch in Indonesia, illustrates the attempts of Europeans to reproduce a replica of the west European city in Southeast Asia.   Thus Jan Peterzoon Coen, the founder of Batavia, planned a replica of a Dutch city, complete with canals and stuffy, tightly packed and many-storeyed houses. As Wertheim comments, Coen '. . . wanted to people the town with a respectable Dutch citizenry as well as to transport to Indonesia the bourgeois character and culture of Holland'.[11] It is not surprising that this attempt to recreate the social structure and town environment of the Dutch town was not successful. The unhealthy physical environment of the stuffy Dutch houses and the malarial canals soon forced the Dutch citizens to move to a more favourable location on the fringes of the city in the suburb of Weltevreden. In addition, the structure of power and administration was scarcely suitable for the duplication of the system of political administration which characterized the Dutch city. The administration of the country was autocratic, not democratic. The centre of the government was the Governor-General's castle, not the town hall. The servants of the Dutch East India Company who made up a considerable proportion of the town's population existed within a strict hierarchical relationship which, while it allowed many of the Dutch to live in the style of 'merchant chiefs' closer to the life of an Eastern noble than a Dutch burgher, did not allow the practice of democracy.

The Dutch society which developed in the new suburb of Weltevreden had all the characteristics of a mestizo ('mixed') culture. The pattern of Dutch life changed from that of the puritanical frugality of bourgeois Holland to an expansive luxurious life concerned with prestige and the emphasis on social occasions. The stuffy Dutch canal houses were replaced by country villas—roomy, airy and cool—surrounded by extensive gardens. The new houses of the Dutch certainly gained some inspiration from the Javanese Priyayi home (aristocratic home), just as the suburb plan of the streets, with a large square and wide roads radiating out from it, was imitative of the Javanese kraton-based cities.[12]

Thus, while in the three centuries following the first significant European contact, the Europeans established many settlements, these centres still remained inferior, both in number, size and importance to the indigenous cities. It is only with the extension of European territorial power in the nineteenth century that the true colonial city—the great primate city—emerged to dominate the urban pattern of Southeast Asia until the present day.

CHAPTER 4

The Emergence of the Colonial City

INTRODUCTION

THE FIRST three centuries of European contact with Southeast Asia were characterized by the establishment of an embryonic colonial urban network; a network of cities that, with the exception of the Philippines and Java, was not intensive, being designed largely to aid the European control of the indigenous Asian trade. This situation was radically changed in the nineteenth century. The need for markets and raw materials for the rapidly industrializing nations of western Europe and the inability of the West Indies to supply enough tropical produce were prime factors in encouraging a shift in colonial emphasis to the tropical lands of Southeast Asia. Additional inducements were provided by improvements in shipping, the opening of the Suez Canal and the political rivalries of the European powers in the area. By the end of the first decade of the twentieth century the territorial division of Southeast Asia had been completed by France, Britain, Holland and the United States. Only Thailand remained independent of colonial rule, but even its rulers were appointing Western advisers to aid the task of modernization.

This expansion of Western control into the area during the nineteenth century involved the creation of a network of urban settlements far in excess of that which had existed in the earlier era. First, and of prime importance, there was the necessity for ports and the establishment of a communications network which linked these ports to the areas of production of the major tropical products or minerals. In conjunction with this a network of administrative centres had to be set up to facilitate political control of the indigenous populations. Finally there was a rapid growth of mining and market towns throughout the colonial territories. While it is the remarkable growth of the large multi-functional port-towns, such as Saigon-Cholon, Singapore, Batavia, Manila, Rangoon and Bangkok, which dominate the pattern of city growth in the nineteenth century, the proliferation of the smaller urban centres should not be ignored because of their important role in helping the colonial machine operate so effectively; the railway junction town, the

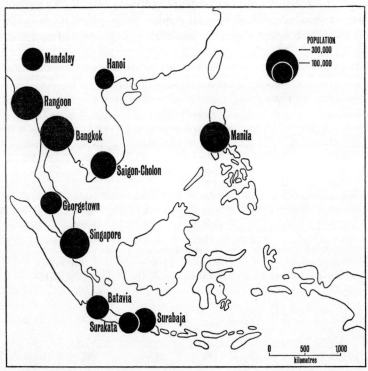

6   The Urban Pattern.   Southeast Asia, c. 1910.   Cities of 100,000 or more in population.

small coastal port, the mining settlement, and the district headquarters enabled the colonial powers to build up their control over the traditional economy and societies of Southeast Asia.   These small centres were the dissemination points of colonial policy, through which the cash economy and the ideas of the West filtered into the countryside.   While the 'primate' port cities of the nineteenth century were largely orientated to the West, these smaller urban centres played an intermediary role between the traditional rural society of Southeast Asia and the rapidly urbanizing societies of western Europe.

The lack of comparative statistics makes it difficult to describe the overall growth of Southeast Asian cities during this era of colonial expansion. In the nineteenth century urban growth was dominated by colonial ports; Singapore, Manila, Rangoon, Batavia and even Bangkok all tripled their populations with the enlargement of their commercial and political functions,

TABLE I

'INDEX OF CENTRALIZATION'

Selected Southeast Asian countries 1910–60; Ratio of first to second largest city.

BURMA (Rangoon)		FRENCH INDOCHINA (Saigon-Cholon)		PHILIPPINES (Manila-Quezon)	
1911	2·1	1911	1·8	1903	5·7
1921	2·3	1921	3·3	1918	6·1
1931	2·7	1931	2·3	1930	3·9
1941	3·0	1939	1·8	1940	4·6
1953	3·9	1955	7·1	1948	6·5
1958	3·9	1960	3·2	1960	5·9

MALAYA AND SINGAPORE (Singapore City)		THAILAND (Bangkok Metropolitan Area)		INDONESIA (Djakarta)	
1911	2·5			1905	1·0
1921	2·9				—
1931	2·9			1930	1·5
1940	—				—
1947	2·7	1947	14·5		—
1957	3·4	1960	25·9	1961	2·9

Sources: Murphey (1957); Sternstein (1965b); Del Tufo (1947).

acting as the 'head-link' between the West and the colonial territory (see Figures 6 and 8). This pre-eminence of one great urban centre—the 'primate city'—continued even into the twentieth century when the number of smaller urban centres were proliferating and acting as alternative attraction centres for the population. For instance, in Java and Madura, two-thirds of the urban population growth between 1905 and 1930

occurred in the six largest towns.[1]   Another example can be
taken from the territories of Malaya and Singapore, which
between 1911 and 1931 increased their number of urban centres
(as defined by the Census) from 92 to 176, while in the same
period Singapore city accounted for a sizeable growth of the
total population.[2]

The urban end-product of this colonial period was the
emergence of a system of cities radically different from the
urban hierarchy of the Western industrialized countries.

As Ginsburg has pointed out,

> Whereas in the United States there is a notable gradation
> of cities from larger to smaller, and only eighteen per cent
> of the urban population lives in cities of one million
> population or more, in Southeast Asia the urban popula-
> tion is most clearly associated with the largest cities.[3]

It is possible to lay too much stress on the growth of these large
urban centres, for there was a considerable growth of secondary
inland centres such as Kuala Lumpur, Hanoi and Surakarta
in the twentieth century.   But as Table 1 shows, the primacy
of the 'great cities' continued to increase, reflecting their
continuing importance as centres of the commercial economy,
political decision, and transport.   By the end of the colonial
era, one great city dominated the urban network of each
country—already a potential 'million city'.

It must be clear from this preceding discussion that any
descriptions of the colonial city will be largely of the features of
'great cities', such as Singapore, Rangoon, Saigon-Cholon,
Manila, Batavia and Bangkok; but the multiplicity of other
colonial urban types should not be forgotten.   Mandalay, the
indigenous 'palace city' took on the function of a colonial
administrative town; Palembang, the oil town; the 'mining-
camp' towns of the Malayan peninsula, the upland resort towns
of the colonialists—all these urban types formed a tremendous
diversity of urban settlements during the colonial era.

What were the principal features of the great primate cities
of this colonial period?   First, they all shared a common
riverine location or coastal site which allowed easy access to

the sea. As Fryer points out the aim of the European founders '. . . was to create economic bases at tidewater, and only later did the administrative function become equally significant'.[4] Amongst the biggest cities the exception to this rule was the city of Bangkok, the only indigenous centre of the large cities; its location so close to the sea was largely arbitrary, decided by the whim of the ruler. Some inland centres such as Surakarta, Bandung, Kuala Lumpur and Hanoi grew substantially in size, but they never assumed the importance of the great cities in the colonial era. Virtually all the great cities, with the exception of Bangkok, were founded on the sites of existing settlements. Saigon was built close to the Chinese village of Cholon founded in 1778; Singapore in the vicinity of a Malay fishing village; Batavia on the site of an already existing trading centre; Manila close by the indigenous Sultanate settlements of Maynila and Tondo, and Rangoon on the site of an important religious shrine and palace town. With the exception of the indigenous centre of Bangkok, all these cities were laid out in a grid-iron pattern and certain areas of the city were set aside for the various racial populations. Despite the careful planning of these cities, the elements of earlier settlement forms did persist to give a distinctive character to the cities. Thus the city of Manila was still dominated by the walled fort and included elements of the old Sultanate settlements in the Tondo area. In Rangoon, the Shwe Dagon Pagoda and the surrounding Buddhist monasteries gave certain parts of the city the appearance of the pre-industrial city. Only Singapore and Saigon could be said to be truly cities of the nineteenth century.

The chief characteristic of these great cities, apart from their considerable size and growth, was their multiplicity of function. The most prominent function of these cities was economic; the colonial city was the 'nerve centre' of colonial exploitation. Concentrated here were the institutions through which capitalism extended its control over the colonial economy—the banks, the agency houses, trading companies, the shipping companies and the insurance companies. For example, in the case of Malaya, Puthucheary shows how the majority of agency houses which had their headquarters in Singapore '. . . retained their more or less complete monopoly of the export-import trade up to about 1920'.[5]   These banks, insurance companies and shipping companies were of course largely European owned.   For instance, in Haiphong, the main port of Hanoi, in 1954 at the time of the armistice all six banks were owned by Europeans.[6]   This is not to deny the importance of alien Asian communities, particularly the Chinese and the Indians in the retail trade which they dominated.   Nor does it ignore the important contribution which the alien communities made to the growth of commerce in the early nineteenth century, particularly through their participation in agricultural and mining schemes.   For instance, the Chinese in both Indo-China and Thailand had a virtual monopoly of the rice-milling industry concentrated in the large cities to which the Europeans never gained control.[7]   But as European trade expanded during the latter half of the nineteenth century, the alien Asian communities' share of import trade began to fall off (except in Thailand) and many Chinese, in particular, began to perform important functions as compradores for the Western import agencies, for their knowledge of the local market proved invaluable to the European firms.

Throughout the colonial era, despite the dominance of alien Asian communities in their populations, the city grew increasingly closer through its economic links to the metropolitan foci of the European colonial powers.   In most cases these great cities were the chief ports of the colonies, handling a high percentage of the imports and exports to and from the colony. The ports of Manila, Singapore, Tandjung Periuk (the port of Batavia), Haiphong, and Rangoon were characterized by a sharp division between the wharves and quays servicing the large ships of the European powers and the mass of smaller jetties which were located in another part of the ports for the indigenous trade.   In terms of the volume and value of trade it was the warehouse and dock areas which were the most important areas of the port for through them passed the greatest volume of goods—Western products and the tropical raw materials for the temperate countries of the Western world.

Thus the smoking chimney stacks of the Western industrial cities were replaced by the long, corrugated-iron godowns (warehouses) of the port city.   The colonial city was essentially an economic intermediary—a middleman—between the metropolitan power and colony. It is not surprising, therefore, that the occupational structure of the cities was characterized by a dominance of the tertiary sector. It was a city of clerks, retailers, administrators, hawkers, retailer merchants and transport workers. The occupational patterns of the colonial city are well illustrated by Rangoon in 1931 where some 62 per cent of the employed population were engaged in commerce, transport, storage, government and other service activities, whereas only 24 per cent were engaged in industry.[8] This pattern with minor modifications was repeated throughout the large cities of Southeast Asia. There was of course some industrial activity in the cities, mainly concerned with the processing of foodstuffs such as rice, sago, sugar and tobacco.[9] Most of the large cities had large workshops for the maintenance of railway equipment, and shipbuilding and repairing facilities. A few cities such as Surabaja and Haiphong had large industrial establishments devoted to the manufacture of textiles and cement respectively.

Whereas in the cities of the Western world the growth of a large tertiary sector has been generally taken as the sign of increasing specialization in urban centres, which is the result of a developing economy, in the context of the Southeast Asian economy of this time, this excessive concentration in the tertiary sector represented an 'unhealthy' trend. It can be argued, of course, that the tertiary-dominant cities of Southeast Asia performed the necessary servicing function of the colonial economy and were thus in no way 'unhealthy' but the consequences of this unbalanced urban structure have been severe for the present-day city. The fact that industrial development was on a small scale prevented employment opportunities in the city from expanding and thus there was a considerable increase in unemployment and under-employment which have persisted until the present day. The proliferation of petty traders, pedicab drivers, footpath astrologers, trinket vendors and food sellers in the colonial city was not a reflection of growing demand, but simply the result of employment opportunities not growing at a fast enough rate to absorb the city population.

A second characteristic of the tertiary occupations of the

colonial city of immense significance was the fact that they came to be overwhelmingly occupied by alien Asian communities. Even in nineteenth-century Bangkok, where the main division was between the Thai *élite* and Thai masses, the

TABLE 2

PERCENT DISTRIBUTION OF MALE EARNING POPULATION
By Economic Function and Selected Races, Rangoon (1931)

ECONOMIC FUNCTION	BURMESE INDIGENOUS	CHINESE	INDIAN	ANGLO-INDIAN	EUROPEAN	TOTAL
Professional and technical experts	4·6	11·3	2·0	1·3	16·7	37·6	2·7
Industrial Managers	0·3	0·3	0·5	0·1	2·4	4·1	0·2
Clerical Workers	12·2	19·1	5·4	4·7	25·2	6·6	6·3
Traders and Shop Assistants	18·7	17·8	43·5	21·2	14·4	18·6	22·4
Craftsmen	30·9	15·4	37·7	13·9	19·3	9·4	18·2
Public Services (not included elsewhere)	0·6	1·4	0·1	(a)	5·8	3·7	0·3
Army, Navy, Air Force and Police	1·7	9·5	0·1	1·3	2·7	9·2	1·5
Rentiers	1·6	2·8	0·6	0·4	5·0	1·5	0·7
Farming, Fishing, Hunting	2·8	2·5	0·8	1·3	(a)	0·1	1·4
Unskilled, semi-skilled labour	25·2	16·0	9·1	55·5	7·2	8·9	45·8
Miscellaneous and insufficiently described	1·4	3·9	0·2	0·3	1·3	0·3	0·5
TOTAL	100·0	100·0	100·0	100·0	100·0	100·0	100·0

Source: Redick (1961), adapted from Census of India 1931, Burma, Vol. XI, Part II, Table VI.
(a) Below 0·05 per cent.

Chinese tended to make up a high proportion of the commercial, artisan and unskilled labour groups which constituted two-thirds of the city's population.[10] A more detailed breakdown of the occupational structure of a colonial city can be shown in the case of Rangoon in 1931 (see Table 2), where the occupational concentration of the various ethnic groups is

59

most marked. The European upper class largely fell into the professional and trading occupations (60 per cent); the Chinese were heavily concentrated in the trading occupations (43 per cent); the Indians made up most of the unskilled labour force; the Anglo-Indians formed an important sector of the clerical and public services as they did in India, and the indigenous community fell into three distinct employment groups—the professional and technical groups, the domestic craftsmen and the unskilled labouring group.[11]

Similar patterns of occupational stratification by ethnic group occurred in all the cities of Southeast Asia in the colonial era. In this situation the vast majority of indigenous inhabitants of the Southeast Asian countries remained engaged in rural occupations, only marginally participating in the economy of the cities. It is true that some of the colonial governments did encourage the indigenous populations, through limited schemes of education, to take government jobs in the cities, but they remained a minority. Within the cities the high degree of occupational specialization which was associated with the various communities (even amongst the various Chinese dialect groups) encouraged a social stratification which in some ways was as rigid as that of the old pre-industrial city.

In addition to the economic functions already elaborated, the great cities were also important centres of the transport network of the colonies. The importance of the role of these cities as ports has been commented upon already, but in addition they were important road and rail, post, telegraph and telephone headquarters, and their position as the foci of the communications network further contributed to their central role in the colonies' development. Most of the large cities—Rangoon, Batavia, Manila, and Singapore were also the centres of colonial administration. One exception to this was French Indo-China where the head of the federal administration, the Governor-General, was located in Hanoi, not the largest urban complex of Saigon-Cholon. An interesting feature of colonial administration was the practice of shifting some government functions to the cool of the hills during the heat of the summer season. This led to the growth of sizeable urban settlements at Baguio in the Philippines and Bogor in Indonesia. Apart from the numerous other educational and cultural functions of these primate cities, they were also the headquarters of the main naval and military bases of the colonial powers.

The controversial question of the role cities play in economic development has already been touched on in the introductory chapter, but it must be considered again at this point because the colonial city has been frequently regarded as playing an inhibitory role in economic development. These cities have been labelled 'parasitic' by Hoselitz[12] because they were the centres from which excessive depletion of natural resources and the exploitation of peasants and primary producers were carried on, thus exerting 'an unfavourable influence on the potentialities of economic growth of the surrounding country'.[13] A situation was created in which the countryside, with the exception of the enclaves of foreign capitalism—mines and plantations—became increasingly impoverished in comparison to the towns. The widespread planting of cash crops brought the rural populations into the sphere of influence of the commercial economy of the cities. The imported manufactured goods which were channelled through the great city to the countryside shattered the domestic industry of the rural areas. Taxes and levies, together with a dangerous dependence on the fluctuating prices of their cash crops on the world market forced the rural farmer into the hands of the middleman and landlord. Finally, the increase of population in the rural areas which occurred as the result of increased political stability and improved medical measures introduced by the colonial powers brought about a growing pressure of population in the rural areas. This view of the Asian city is echoed even by contemporary writers . . .

> Cities are parasitic on the rural areas—they draw the food products and send back the manufactured commodities, they suck out the sturdy, healthy stock from the villages and sterilize it into a race of weak neurotic dregs. Cities are dysgenic.[14]

Even in Bangkok, where the relationship between city and countryside represented an indigenous cultural tradition, the penetration of capitalist elements in the nineteenth century helped this process of alienation between city and countryside.

Ideally, Hoselitz argues, this parasitic phase of colonial city development should only be temporary, for

> ... the divergent trends of economic development within these cities and outside them, in the wider countryside, had the effect of creating a situation which tended to counteract and eventually turn the parasitic impact of these cities into its opposite.[15]

The growing differential in income between city and countryside would attract the rural migrant to the city and help create a work force committed to urban employment, allowing industry to be established. Once industry had started, this in turn would have a favourable influence on the countryside and the end result would be growing economic development within the whole country.

In fact the structure of the colonial economy of Southeast Asia did not permit the cities to be 'generative' of economic growth. The colonial city still remained economically subordinate to the metropolis and world trade. The colonial city, to use Weber's dual classification, was neither 'consumer city', claiming food from the countryside and offering little but political stability in return, nor was it a 'producer city', exchanging its manufactured goods for food.[16] Rather the great cities of Southeast Asia were intermediate between these two polar types, acting as the foci for the alien middleman in the economy of these countries. It is hardly surprising, therefore, that the colonial city's overall effect was to inhibit economic growth. Of course it may be argued that the colonial cities of Southeast Asia were 'generative' of economic growth, in that they were the institutional integrators of the colonies in systems of international trade. And certainly it cannot be denied, as some authorities point out, that 'Foreign trade is vital as a method of obtaining the initial finance, particularly the foreign exchange, required to support the process of growth. . . .'[17] But the colonial economy did not allow these earnings to be invested in such a manner as to aid economic growth, except indirectly through the colonial governments, and consequently the cities never played a 'generative' role in economic development in the ideal manner described by Hoselitz.

The great city's role in the social, political and cultural development of these countries was no less significant. Not only because, with the exception of Bangkok, they were cultural importations from abroad, but because the actual process of transplanting these urban forms into the non-Western countries represents the cultural diffusion . . . of man's most complex artifact—the modern city'.[18] The culture, way of life and population of the city were alien to the way of life of the indigenous inhabitants. The cities were populated by a mixed and culturally heterogenetic population, the majority of whom were immigrants from outside the country. Rangoon in the nineteen-thirties had a dominance of Indians; Singapore and Bangkok dominantly Chinese populations, while the cities of Manila, Batavia and Saigon had smaller Chinese communities. It was, however, the Europeans, despite their small proportion of the total city population, who were the most clearly defined social group at the top of the social scale. The colonial city may not have been a city heavily populated by Europeans, but it was a city run for the convenience of Europeans. The European residents of the colonial city, clearly demarcated by the colour of their skin, their superior position in the social hierarchy, and their responsibility as colonial rulers, lived in encapsulated communities segregated from the major part of the city's population. The European community of the colonial city was as closed and tight-knit as any Asian village. The spacious residences of the European community, their clubs, the golf and race-courses, remain a permanent part of the morphology of the contemporary city.

The alien Asian communities of the cities were no less segregated, both residentially and occupationally, although they tended to mix much more in the market places. The contribution of these alien Asian groups to the task of building the modern brick buildings of the great cities was immense, particularly in the second half of the nineteenth century. The smallest communities of the colonial city were generally the indigenous groups who could be divided into two clearly demarcated social groups. First what might be labelled the 'co-operating *élites*', those elements of the traditional aristocracy who were working with the colonial rulers; and secondly, the poor indigenous population who were working in marginal occupations such as hawking and unskilled labour.

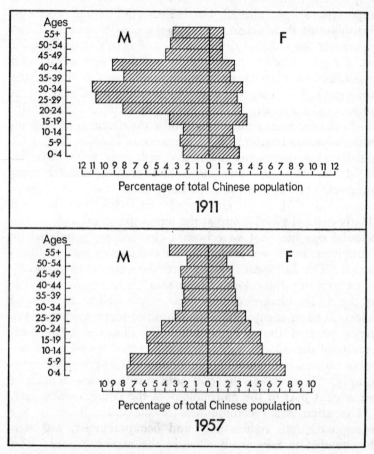

7   Age structure diagrams of Kuala Lumpur city Chinese, 1911 and 1957.

Thus while it cannot be denied that the city acted as a cultural filter through which elements of Westernization entered the colonies, the structure of colonial society inhibited widespread social change.   Only the small educated Westernized *élite* of indigenous population which began to emerge in the city really felt the full-scale impact of Westernization, but their political influence was comparatively small, except in the Philippines and Indonesia, until after the Japanese invasions. It was generally in the cities that the colonial powers made the first tentative gestures towards political emancipation, setting up town councils which offered some sort of representation to the city populations. It was in the cities too, that the majority of indigenous literary movements, which were associated with the *élite* nationalism of the city-based groups grew up. Rizal wrote in Europe, but it was his translations in Tagalog which were circulated in Manila and aroused the enthusiasm of the Filipino nationalists.[19] The first vernacular newspapers began in these great cities broadcasting the ideas of nationalism and freedom from the colonial rulers.

Together with the social structure and alien culture, the demographic character of the colonial city also contributed to its failure to act as a generator of overall cultural change. The population was largely transitory and heavily weighted in favour of males; the cities were essentially pioneer cities in which the populations intended to stay only for a limited period and thus they had a limited interest in developing a knowledge of the country in which they were staying (see Figure 7). Exceptions to this were some of the colonial administrators who did take a deep interest in the indigenous society. Above all, the colonial city was culturally alien from the rest of the country, and inhibitive of cultural change.

The morphology of the colonial cities reflects this diverse economic, ethnic, social and political structure which has been described above. While all the great cities shared certain common features in their internal patterns—the universal Western commercial district, the Chinatown and rural-like compounds of the indigenous dwellers, there was enough variation in the manner in which Western urban forms were established and related to existing urban settlements to broadly differentiate three main types of town on the basis of the internal distribution patterns which emerged. First, there were the towns which were founded as pre-industrial settlements which, with the advent of colonial rule began to change their character, with the grafting on of Western urban forms. Rangoon, Mandalay and Hué were examples of this type of urban settlement. Secondly, there were the 'planned' Western settlements, such as Singapore, which grew up completely away from the pre-industrial settlements and incorporated elements of planning from other colonial areas and the West. Finally, there were the indigenous settlements, such as Bangkok

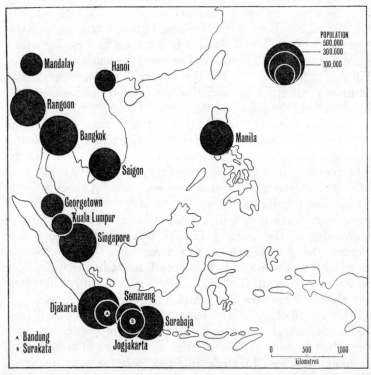

8   The Urban Pattern.   Southeast Asia, c. 1930.   Cities of 100,000 or more.

and Luang Prabang which, despite Western influences, still retained their basic character as indigenous cities for much of the colonial period.   The following section discusses three examples of these types of city: Rangoon, the grafted city; Singapore, the planned city; and Bangkok, the indigenous city.

THE GRAFTED CITY—*Rangoon*

The pre-colonial history of Rangoon can be summed up briefly. Rangoon was founded on the site of a fishing village at the confluence of the Hlaing and Pegu Rivers by the great Burmese leader, Alaungpaya, in the mid-eighteenth century. Before this the site had been significant, largely because of the presence of the Buddhist shrine—the Shwe Dagon, and it seems likely that its presence here encouraged the Burmese leader to choose this site. During much of the period prior to 1826, Alaungpaya's Rangoon remained largely a trading port, exporting teak as well as building merchant ships. After 1826, the town suffered a decline for the annexation of the Arakan and Tenasserim by the British cut off a great deal of the town's trade. This decline greatly aided the British in the planning of Rangoon. These plans were also helped by the fact that the Burmese King had the pre-industrial town shifted a mile and a half inland to the slopes of the Shwe Dagon hill in order to give him greater protection against the Europeans. After the British annexed lower Burma in 1852, they were able to design what was in effect a new town but they still planned it around existing pre-industrial elements of the old town. The British orientated the city around the Sule Pagoda, a minor pagoda to the west of the old Burmese town. Here they planned the government commercial centre, stretching out in a series of blocks, spreading away from the main waterfront road. A great part of the river frontage was soon occupied by rice mills, teak wharves, and the other storage facilities of the colonial port. A typical colonial town, the chief orientation of Rangoon was towards the port and the commercial centre of the city. The area to the north where the Burmese city had been shifted became the cantonment area, and for some time the Shwe Dagon Pagoda was surrounded by a rampart and used as a military strong point. The high terrace to the south-west of the pagoda was developed as a European quarter with large compounds, clubs, official residences, and many open spaces.

The city grew rapidly. Within three years of its foundation it was estimated to have 46,000 inhabitants. By 1872 this figure had reached 92,000, and by 1931, it had risen to 400,000. This rapid population growth also saw a remarkable change in the population composition. During the period between 1852 and 1872 the Burmese made up approximately 75 per cent of the population, but by 1911, the Burman's percentage had dropped to 31 per cent, and the Indians increased to over 50 per cent. Thus Rangoon rapidly assumed the characteristic of an alien centre. The rapid growth in population in this period also saw an increasing complexity in the social ecology of the city; the racial components of the city tended to concentrate in markedly different areas.

Spate and Trueblood have described in some detail the ecological patterns of Rangoon in 1931.[20] The European commercial core of the city was located in the block surrounding Sule Pagoda. Here were the Customs House, the Post and Telegraph offices, the lower court, Reserve Bank, City Hall and other administrative buildings as well as the large bank and trading houses. Interpenetrating this area, and to the west of it were located the smaller firms of the Indian and Chinese. Here too were the bazaars and markets, the street hawker and the food seller. This was the Asian commercial business area. In this area were located the highest densities of the city, sometimes reaching as much as 100,000 people per square mile. East of the administrative commercial core were the Burma Secretariat buildings and a residential area of lower middle-class Indians and Anglo-Indians. Farther to the east on Monkey Point, and along the shores of the Pazundaung Creek were the rice mills, sawmills, shipbuilding establishments and much of the city's industry. This most highly urbanized part of the city was clearly separated from the outer suburbs by the railway which ran to the north of the inner city area. To the north of the city was located an area which Spate labels a 'fossil area', in which were the Shwe Dagon Pagoda and the open space formerly occupied by the British military cantonment.

There were three main residential zones. First, the shop house dwellers of the inner city who were largely Indian and Chinese; secondly, the inner-suburban residential areas which encircled the city and fell into three distinctly different sectors;

in the Theinbyu East circle, the most wretched slums of
Rangoon were found occupied by 'dhobis' (washermen) and
other poor Indian inhabitants; next to it, in the Theinbyu West
Circle was an area of large but closely-built houses mostly
occupied by Anglo-Indians; and finally on the elevated Rose
Bank Terrace where Government House was located, the
European clubs, and much of the first-class housing of the
Europeans, were laid out in spacious compounds. This dense
pattern of the inner suburbs was repeated in the outer fringes
of the city (the European settlement tending to follow the high
ridges) where the immigrant and Burmese groups concentrated
on the low-lying areas close to the river. One unique area on
the fringe of the city between the Windermere Terrace Ridge
and the Hlaing River, was the Kemmendine district which
Spate and Trueblood describe as a huge Burmese village.
Within the village were located distinctly Burmese industries
such as cheroot rolling, gem polishing, boat building, and
umbrella making. The suburb had the appearance of a large
rural village; 'The streets are village streets, the houses not
much more substantial than village huts, well shaded and often
with verandahs half screened by flowering shrubs.'[21] Finally,
outside the city borders there was the inevitable market-
gardening belt, largely in the hands of the Chinese, although
some animal rearing was carried on by Indians.

While it is clear that by 1931 the ecology of Rangoon was
largely governed by its development as a colonial economic and
administrative centre, and by the British replanning of the city,
the city morphology still incorporated enough elements of its
pre-industrial past to justify the title, 'grafted colonial city'.

A PLANNED COLONIAL CITY—Singapore

When Sir Stamford Raffles founded Singapore city in 1819,
there was a population of some 150 fishermen. By 1947 this
figure had grown to over 600,000, the majority of whom were
alien Chinese immigrants. From the very beginning, Raffles
showed great imagination in the planning of a town which was
architecturally adapted to the tropical climate and, more
important, its basic plans were designed to incorporate an
extremely mixed population. The original layout of ethnic

quarters is illustrated in the accompanying Figure 9. In the original plan the European town and government area covered the largest area of town occupying a well-drained and high

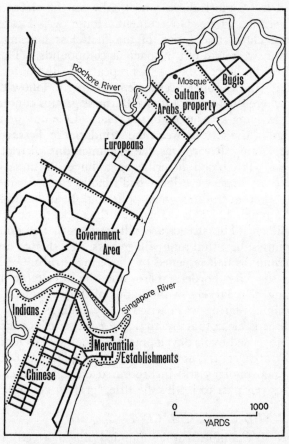

9 Proposed racial groupings in Singapore city, 1828.

site between Rochore River and Singapore River, and including the area of Fort Canning Hill which contained the military cantonment. The Arabs and Bugis were located close to the Malay Sultan's compound and the mosque, and the remainder of the local Malays whom Raffles assumed would be mainly concerned with fishing were intended to dwell along the northern fringes of the Rochore River. The two largest alien communities, the Chinese and the Indians, were located to the south of the Singapore River, adjacent to the mercantile and commercial business district of Raffles Place. The potential rowdiness and disturbances of the Chinese and Indian immigrants was separated from the quietness of the spacious European area by the Singapore River. The European town was laid out with all the integral institutions of the English Colonial city—the cricket ground, the church, the government buildings, the club, and the military cantonment, were all incorporated in this area close to the large and spacious dwellings of the Europeans.[22]

During the nineteenth century as Singapore's importance and wealth grew, largely as a reflection of its role as an entrepôt port, its population increased rapidly. This increase was largely of Chinese, but there was also an increase in foreign-born Malaysians. Not surprisingly, this rapid increase in population produced some changes in the ecology of the city. First, population growth forced the city to expand outside its original boundaries. In a like manner to Batavia, the pressure of the population in the inner city began to force the Europeans to move into outer suburbs such as Tanglin, where they built houses in a much more gracious style not dissimilar to those of the Dutch in Batavia. The area to which they moved, set in rolling hills, was one of the most healthy areas in Singapore. The houses they built showed special adaptation of European architectural styles to the tropical conditions; the roofs had a wide overhang to protect the houses from the sun and rain; glass windows were replaced by slotted shutters which allowed the wind to circulate; and the verandahs were large, commonly serving as living rooms. The rooms within the house were large and each was equipped with a 'punkah' and later an electric fan. Finally there were numerous outbuildings to accommodate the many servants who worked for the European masters.[23] The life of the Europeans in Singapore was remarkably imitative of the aristocratic life in England, centring around elaborate entertaining, garden parties, club membership, and tremendous concern with social status.[24]

Despite the Europeans' political and social dominance, by 1901 Singapore was in all other respects a Chinese city. While the majority of Chinese were concentrated in the already over-crowded Chinatown, originally laid out by Raffles, some had already begun to move to the north of the town in areas which had formerly been occupied by the Europeans. The Indian community had already begun to spread beyond their original Indian area to the north of Chinatown, and to areas north of the original Malay areas. The Malay, Bugis and Arab community had remained remarkably concentrated despite a considerable increase in their population.[25] What is remarkable is that the basic patterns of ethnic distribution laid out in Singapore's original plan, still persisted to such a considerable extent, even though the city population had grown so dramatically.

In 1947 the basic patterns of ethnic distribution still persisted along the lines of the original planned town, clearly shown in the sequence of maps in Hodder's article.[26] Singapore remained a city planned by Europeans, and inhabited by non-Europeans whose residential distribution continued to reflect the intentions of the European rulers to an amazing degree.

THE INDIGENOUS 'COLONIAL CITY'—*Bangkok*

Bangkok was unique in this period of colonial city growth because it was never under colonial control. Nevertheless, while its power structure and to some extent its social structure still retained elements of the patterns of the pre-industrial city, as revealed in the city's morphology, the increasing impact of capitalism began to change the economic functions of the city, and resulted in the emergence of what may be labelled a dual city—the old pre-industrial palace city and the commercial city.

Bangkok was founded in 1767 by the Thai King, Phya Tak, who had been defeated at Ayuthia by the Burmese. In what must have been a similar process to the creation of Mandalay, except that it was precipitated by a more genuine loss of power, he founded the walled city of Bangkok on the site of the present Regent's Palace at Thonburi, on the west bank of the river. It was not until the reign of King Rama I (1782–1809) that the true pattern of pre-industrial Bangkok began to take shape. Hall describes how 'Rama I built himself a palace on the opposite side of the river at Bangkok proper and surrounded it with a double line of fortifications, and there

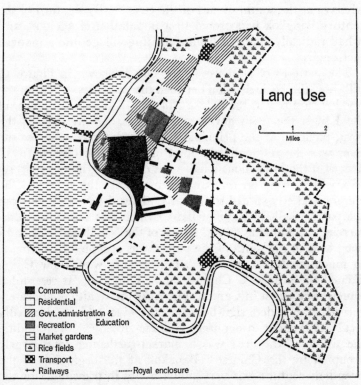

Land Use

0   1   2
Miles

Commercial
Residential
Govt. administration & Education
Recreation
Market gardens
Rice fields
Transport
Railways   ------Royal enclosure

10   Major Land-use patterns in the Bangkok Metropolitan area, 1960.

under the shelter of the outer wall the present city began to arise.'[27] He stabilized the administration of the provinces and strengthened the central government. Under King Monkut, 1850–68, the commercial city grew rapidly, especially after the conclusion of the Treaty of Friendship and Commerce with Britain in 1855 which opened the way to trade with this and other nations. Monkut also used Europeans as advisers to the government and built roads and canals, but it was primarily under the reigns of Kings Rama IV and VI that two Bangkoks emerged. Sommerville, writing at the end of the nineteenth century describes the growth of the commercial city, 'During the last thirty years the colonialists with mercantile enterprise have established godowns (warehouses), shipping houses, and wharves at the southern end of the city.'[28] By the turn of the century Bangkok had grown to a population of 350,000, and it had radically changed from a floating village into a modern metropolis.

The patterns of land use in the city as shown in Figure 12 still show this basic division between the two cities. Within the royal enclosure was the palace (the centre of political power of the King), the main government offices, the law courts, the royal palace and the principal Buddhist temples. Across the river was the residential adjunct of the palace city; the residences of the indigenous Thai; rows of floating houses built on pontoons floating on the canals which were the streets. The commercial city spread southwards along the New Road from the palace walls to the east bank, which was the major commercial and banking area. Much of the New Road and Sampeng area to the south of the palace was occupied by Chinese; so much so that European commentators who knew China likened the area to a Chinese city. One said, 'It resembled somewhat a street in Canton, but lacks the wealth, elaborately carved and gilded sign-boards, that give such a decidedly local atmosphere to a purely Chinese street.'[29] Surrounding the whole of the area was a market-gardening zone largely occupied by the Chinese. Bangkok at the beginning of the twentieth century was very much a city in transition, for the indigenous city and the newer elements of the commercial city coexisted rather than one dominating the other.

CONCLUSION

This brief review of the features of colonial urbanization has emphasized the importance of this period to the present-day urban patterns. The basic problems of colonial urbanization —the parasitic great cities, characterized by excessive concentration of the colonies' political and economic activities;

warped occupational structures and socially and culturally alien populations—have persisted despite the end of the colonial system which bred them. The emergence of the new nations of Southeast Asia from this period of colonialism should have given the new rulers the opportunity to remedy these problems. But can the new city-bred rulers of Southeast Asia solve the problems of colonial urbanism when they themselves are a product of the very environment which they must seek to change?

CHAPTER 5

Modern Cult Centres: The Southeast Asian City today

WITHOUT QUESTION the most important influences on the pattern of postwar urbanization in Southeast Asia have been the process of decolonization and the growth of nationalism which have accompanied the emergence of the new nations of Southeast Asia. Ideally, the Southeast Asian cities should have thrown off the parasitic role of the colonial period and should now be playing a generative role in the economic, political and social development of the new nations. This chapter describes the growth of various cities in Southeast Asia since 1945 and attempts to evaluate the role that these cities are actually playing at the present stage of nation state development.

Since 1945 the urban areas of Southeast Asia appear to have been growing at a much faster rate than the total population. However, there is reason to believe that these figures of urban growth may be inflated. The majority of statistics are taken from government publications which adopt widely different criteria for their definitions of 'urban population', making the comparison and assessment of 'city growth rates' and 'levels of urbanization' exceptionally difficult amongst the various countries. Some countries, such as Malaya, adopt a purely statistical definition, including all gazetted areas of over 1,000 in population as urban. Other countries, such as the Philippines, choose to define urban places on the basis of a political definition. Here the practice of establishing chartered cities allows them to be placed directly under the administrative control of the President of the Republic, thus taking power away from the provincial governor. In practice many of the cities which were to be granted charters were so small in size that it was necessary to enlarge the area, thus taking in '. . . large sectors of rural territory containing outlying villages and towns and taxable farmlands'.[1] Thus many of the chartered cities of the Philippines classified as urban actually have substantial rural populations. Spencer, after a careful analysis of the boundaries of these chartered cities in relation to their built-up urban areas, concluded that the urban population in 1948 was over-enumerated by almost 25 per cent.[2] At the other extreme in some Southeast Asian countries the urban population has grown so rapidly in the postwar era that it has spread outwards beyond existing city boundaries. Thus the percentage of urban population in Singapore actually fell from 72·5 per cent in 1947 to 63·1 per cent in 1957.[3] This was not a reflection of a decline in the urban population but of the fact that some urban population was now living in areas defined as rural by the census. The problems of arriving at accurate statements on the rates of city growth and the levels of urbanization are almost insurmountable at present, and can only be solved if some common urban definition is introduced throughout the region.

Such a definition will have to depend on a common agreement being reached concerning the difficult question of what constitutes urban as opposed to rural life. Western writers have attempted to grapple with the problem by suggesting that certain significant features of urban behaviour stem from concentration of population in centres of certain size with a high density and heterogeneous composition of population.[4] Gourou[5] has dismissed the first two of these criteria in a discussion of the problems of defining a city in French Indo-china. He illustrates the inadequacy of size as a criteria pointing out that many of the towns of the Tonkin delta often have only 500 inhabitants while rural villages sometimes exceed 10,000 in population. In addition, rural densities in the same area often exceeded 2,000 people per square mile, greatly exceeding urban densities. The heterogeneity of population was the only valid criterion since the cities of Tonkin contained largely alien inhabitants at this time. It would appear that the only valid definition must rest on the proportion of population engaged in non-agricultural activities, but this is difficult

77

to apply in the Southeast Asian context because of the lack of adequate statistics.

TABLE 3

PROPORTION OF URBAN TO TOTAL POPULATION
In selected Southeast Asian countries *circa* 1960

Country	Year	Percentage Urban
Brunei	1960	43·6
Cambodia	1958	12·8
Indonesia	1961	14·8
Malaysia Federation of Malaya	1957	42·8
North Borneo	1960	14·9
Sarawak	1960	15·0
Singapore	1960	62·6
Philippines	1960	29·9
Thailand	1960	12·5
Australia	1961	81·9
New Zealand	1961	74·0
England and Wales	1961	80·0
France	1954	55·9
United States	1960	69·9

Sources U.N.O. 'Report on the Asian Population Conference' (1964); Selected statistical publications of the various countries.

Note: This table shows proportion urban as defined by the respective countries.

Despite these statistical problems, the patterns of city growth and urbanization (i.e. the proportion of total population resident in cities) can be described in general terms for Southeast Asia in the postwar period. The overall levels of urbanization for the various countries as shown in Table 3, indicate striking contrasts amongst countries. The proportion of the total population resident in urban places as defined by the different countries ranges from figures of below 15 per cent in Cambodia, the Borneo territories, and Indonesia, to 30 per cent in the Philippines and over 40 per cent in Malaya. Only in the two small countries of Singapore and Brunei does the level of urbanization compare with the Western countries. It must be remembered that the recorded 'levels' of urbanization are based on each country's assessment of its 'urban' population and that there are dangers in accepting such definitions.[6]

A more realistic assessment can be made on the basis of population resident in places of 20,000 or more, and while data is not available for all the Southeast Asian countries, Table 4 does indicate that the assessments of the Southeast Asian countries are inflated if some common statistical base is accepted. Thus Burma emerges with one of the lowest levels of urbanization in the whole of Southeast Asia and the Philippines figure is substantially deflated. This table also records the yearly growth rates of urban population as compared to total population, and while it shows that the urban areas have been growing at a considerably faster rate than the total population, the overall level of urbanization has not increased sizeably except in Sarawak.

TABLE 4

CHANGES IN THE PROPORTION OF POPULATION
In localities of 20,000 or more in selected Southeast Asian countries

Country	Dates	Percentage of Total Population in Centres 20,000 +	Percent Yearly Increase of Centres 20,000 +	Percent Yearly Increase Total Population
Federation of Malaya	1947	17·1		
	1957	20·8	5·8	2·8
Sarawak	1947	6·9		
	1957	10·7	11·0	3·6
Philippines	1950	12·7		
	1960	14·2	5·3	4·0
Indonesia	1950	9·1		
	1960	11·2	5·3	2·4
Thailand	1947	5·1		
	1960	8·8	12·0	3·5

Sources: Fell (1960); Hamzah (1964); Sternstein (1965b); Hauser (1957); Biro Pusat Statistik (1962); U.N.O., 'Demographic Yearbook 1960' (1960).

As Ginsburg has commented with respect to the area, 'The percentage of total population classified as urban is in general so low and the normal rates of population increase so high that the growth of urban population *as a percentage of total population* has not been spectacular'.[7] Thus there seems some evidence that the countries of Southeast Asia are passing through a phase of 'pseudo urbanization' in common with many other Third World countries.

If these rates of urban growth in the Southeast Asian countries are calculated by urban size categories it does suggest that the largest sized city groupings (above 100,000) have not been growing as fast as some of the smaller sized groupings in the postwar era. At first sight this might seem to indicate the beginnings of a more balanced urban hierarchy indicative of economic development, but actually it occurred because of two trends which have masked the fact that the great cities of Southeast Asia are absorbing as substantial a proportion of the urban population increase, as they did in the colonial era. First, there is the growing suburbanization of the great cities which has not always been recorded in the statistics; and, secondly, the smaller cities are accumulating population on a smaller base and thus their growth rates are higher (see Figure 11).

However, it is only when the growth rates of the individual cities are compared that the supposedly booming rates of urban growth emerge. In particular it is the largest metropolitan areas which are growing at rates greatly in excess of the other individual cities. Thus if the rates of growth of the first and second largest cities in selected Southeast Asian countries are compared (see Table 5), it is obvious that in most cases the larger city is growing almost one-third faster than the second city.

The only exception to this general pattern occurs in the cases where, with independence, the larger colonial political units have been split up into smaller countries, and the capitals of the new countries have been growing faster than the old colonial capitals. Thus Kuala Lumpur has grown at almost double the rate of Singapore in the postwar period, reflecting its position as the capital of the new state of Malaysia. Similarly, Phnom-Penh has grown rapidly as the capital of independent Cambodia compared to the former capital of French Indochina,

Hanoi. In some cases the improvements in the regional economy and transportation have aided the second city's growth. Such a case is the port city of Cebu in the Philippines[8] which has grown substantially in the postwar period. But, overall, the dominance and importance of the great primate city does not seem to have diminished since the colonial era.

TABLE 5

PERCENTAGE AND TOTAL POPULATION INCREASES
In largest and second largest cities for selected Southeast Asian countries

Country and City	Date Population	Annual Percent Increase	Date Population
CAMBODIA	1936		1960
Phnom-Penh	103,000	14·0	450,000
Battembang	20,000	3·2	35,526
THAILAND	1947		1960
Bangkok Met. Area	781,662	8·3	1,633,346
Chengmai	38,211	5·5	65,736
PHILIPPINES	1948		1960
Manila Met. Area	1,366,840	4·6	2,135,705
Cebu	167,503	4·1	251,146
INDONESIA	1931		1961
Djakarta	533,015	15·2	2,933,052
Surabaya	341,675	6·5	1,007,945
FEDERATION OF MALAYA			
AND SINGAPORE	1947		1957
Singapore city	680,000	3·4	912,300
Kuala Lumpur	176,000	7·9	316,200

Sources: Indo-China (1943); Sternstein (1965b); Philippines Census 1960. Summary Report (1963); Withington (1963); Fell (1960); Chua (1960); Cambodian Census 1959 (1959).

There is very little available evidence on what has been the main contribution to this considerable increase in urban populations. Cities grow in three ways: (1) through boundary extension, (2) through in-migration, and (3) by natural increase. Most evidence indicates that the last two demographic forces have been the major causes of city growth. Certainly some of the Southeast Asian large cities have expanded their boundaries during the postwar period. Thus, for instance, Kuala Lumpur enlarged its area from eighteen square miles to thirty square miles between 1947 and 1957, and in the process incorporated new villages which were adjacent to the city. Another example is Bangkok which grew in size from 49·5 square kilometres to 124·7 square kilometres between 1947 and 1960. At the same time the growth of satellite towns and suburbs outside city boundaries such as Petaling Jaya near Kuala Lumpur city, the new housing developments outside Singapore city and the Quezon city area on the fringes of Manila city, the majority of which have populations working in the main city, have not always been included in the total urban increase. Ringing many of these cities are the squatter colonies, illegally occupying land outside municipal control. Ideally these populations should also be classified with the city population, for what income they earn comes largely from city employment. If all these areas outside the city boundaries had been included, the 'great city' population figures would be much higher.

The contribution of natural increase is even more difficult to ascertain, for comprehensive data on rural-urban differentials in mortality and fertility do not exist for the majority of the countries of the region. Some evidence from Singapore, which shows a slight decline in crude birth-rates in the last twenty years, seems to suggest that fertility in the Malaysian area may be lower in the cities than in rural areas, but the availability of data from other cities and countries is not enough to ascertain whether this pattern is repeated in other cities. The difficult question of whether fertility decreases as urbanization increases, as it did in the West, is as yet unproven in the Southeast Asian context. Certainly the crowded urban milieu with its great shortage of housing would seem to discourage having children, and the superior communications of the city should aid any propaganda in favour of birth control. But the traditional social attitudes of the Southeast Asian people still favour large families, for children represent a form of social security in old age. There is little doubt, however, that the improved medical conditions have led to a substantial drop in crude death-rates and infant mortality rates. Thus in Singapore the crude death-rate has fallen from 24·2 per 1,000 population in 1931 to 6·4 in 1959. The infant mortality rate has fallen considerably more, from 191·3 per 1,000 live births in 1931 to 36 per 1,000 in 1959. Compare this with the rate of crude deaths of Malays who are largely rural dwellers, which even in the more urbanized states of Perak, Selangor and Negri Sembilan fell only from 25·4 per 1,000 in 1921 to 19·1 per 1,000 in 1948.[9] Evidence for repetitive mortality patterns in other Southeast Asian cities is not readily available, but if they do follow this pattern, the substantial decline in mortality would certainly have accounted for a considerable natural increase in city populations.

Although there is doubt about what proportion of recent population growth in the urban areas has been caused by natural increase and boundary extension, there is no question that rural-urban migration has been a most important contributor to city growth. Even at the initial period of their growth, the majority of Southeast Asian cities had been peopled by rural migrants from other countries, particularly the Chinese who came principally from the rural areas of South China.[10] Yet these rural migrants adapted surprisingly well to the urban environment and rapidly assumed a position of numerical and commercial dominance in the city. However, the postwar assumption of political independence has put an end to this alien immigration and created a situation where the psychological, political and employment patterns existing in the city are more favourable for the indigenous inhabitants. This situation, when it is associated with the problems of rural society, in which the indigenous inhabitants have been concentrated in the colonial era, has been one fact encouraging the indigenes to move to the city in much greater numbers.

Virtually every country in Southeast Asia is now experiencing a rapid rural-urban movement. The 'place of birth' figures of city dwellers, although not always indicative of whether a person lived in the country or a small town before he moved to the city, are revealing in this respect. Thus, in a survey carried out in Djakarta in 1954, 74 per cent of the Indonesian household heads interviewed had been born outside the city,[11] while most recent censuses for the Philippines,

Cambodia and Thailand record percentages of 46·9, 47·7 and 26·6 per cent respectively. It thus can be argued justifiably that many of the cities of Southeast Asia deserved to be classified as 'migrant cities' to adopt Taeuber's definition.[12] While much of this migration has been motivated by the problems of the countryside, there are other factors operating to draw the people to the cities. One of the most important of these has been the political insecurity in the countryside which has accompanied the attempts of the new rulers to ensure their countries' independence and security. For instance, the political instability which has resulted from the rebel movements in Malaya, Vietnam and Burma has brought about a massive influx of rural refugees to the main cities of these countries. In some places the people have been forcibly removed from the rural areas, as was the case in Malaya, and shifted to newly-created 'new-villages'. In Burma the movement has been much more spontaneous, and the people have flocked to the large cities of Mandalay and Rangoon. In some cases, political instability has the reverse effect for it is reported that American bombing in North Vietnam has caused a mass evacuation of women and children from the cities.

It has been customary for researchers into rural-urban migration to classify the motivations bringing about this process within a push-pull framework. Their conclusions have generally been that it is the 'push' factors which are the more significant in forcing the rural migrant into the city. These conclusions are in direct contrast to the experience of the industrial revolution in western Europe, where there was a close connection between the demands for labour exerted by the rapidly growing industry in the cities, and the tendency for agricultural production and techniques to reduce the demand for farm labour and to increase the food supply to the cities. Thus there was an even balance between the push and pull circumstances of migration. In Southeast Asia it would appear that people are being forced into the cities by the unstable political and economic conditions in the countryside and there are not the same attracting forces operating in the city. This has led to the persistence of the economic problems of the city already discussed in relation to the colonial city, for the rural migrants have been forced to move into the city's already over-inflated tertiary sector, where they find it difficult to earn an adequate living. Rural migrants come to the city to alleviate their rural poverty, only to find it is replaced by urban poverty.[13]

THE ECONOMIC PATTERNS OF THE SOUTHEAST ASIAN CITY

Although the economic features of the colonial city have already been discussed, a brief recapitulation of the major features is an aid to our understanding of the economic structure of the contemporary Southeast Asian cities. The period of colonialism was a period of commercial urbanization which created a series of cities (largely on the seacoast) for the purpose of collection, storing, handling, and distribution of exports and imports. Some processing of raw materials such as rubber, rice, and jute did occur in these centres but there was little development of major industry. The process of urbanization under colonialism did not entirely concentrate city growth in the large coastal centres. There were also some secondary inland centres of extractive industries, such as the tin-mining centres of Malaya, transport industries, and administrative centres. The most ubiquitous colonial urban settlement, however, was the service centre, concentrating largely on commercial and servicing functions.

There can be little doubt that the independence of the Southeast Asian countries has ushered in new attitudes towards economic development. Certainly the economic policies of the Southeast Asian countries vary widely. They range from the socialist-planning of North Vietnam to the capitalist societies of Malaysia and the Philippines, but whatever the strategy or ideology of economic development, there is one element that all have in common: this is the desire to achieve a balanced economic development in order to correct the unbalanced economy persisting from the colonial period. In general this means that these countries put forward economic development policies which emphasize the role of industrialization. Theoretically, such industrialization policies should bring about a completely new pattern of urban centres.

85

But for various reasons the growth of industrialization in Southeast Asia in the postwar period has not been as rapid as the countries would desire. In part this is attributable to the difficulty of imposing political unity and creating conditions of stability; the difficulty in encouraging investment, both from within the countries and outside; and the lack of skilled and trained workers for industry. Theoretically at least, the introduction of the industrialization programmes advocated for the region should do two things to the pattern of urbanization in the area. First, it should lead to a wider spread of industrial centres because certain active locational features of industrialization should crystallize around the raw material and power sources previously under-developed or used only as raw materials for export. Secondly, it should tend to create more industry in the already existing city areas, where the labour and consumer markets already exist. These changes should result in a twofold growth in the pattern of cities: (1) the growth of single-function cities such as iron and steel centres or aluminium works, and (2) the diversification of the occupational structure of the larger cities.

There is some evidence that the former of these changes has progressed considerably in the socialist society of North Vietnam where an engineering complex has been established at Thai Nguyen and Nam Dinh and light industrial centres at Viet Tri and other centres. In Cambodia some small industrial units have been established in existing towns outside the capital Phnom-Penh.[14] In other parts of Southeast Asia the creation of new industrial centres has been sluggish, although the Maria Christina hydro-electric project implemented by the Filipino government is now providing power for a new centre of heavy industries in Iligan town in the island of Mindanao, hitherto one of the least developed and urbanized regions. Another scheme which should, when it is fully implemented, lead to the creation of a new industrial centre, is the Asahan power scheme in Sumatra which will provide power for an aluminium works and associated industries at Belawan.

In fact the political situation has been a more important influence on the creation of new towns than industrial development. Thus the breakup of the old colonial units such as

86

Singapore and Malaya and French Indochina, has meant that the newly independent states such as Malaya and Cambodia have attempted to break down their former dependence on the ports of Singapore or Saigon-Cholon by creating a new port in the case of Cambodia, and upgrading Port Swettenham some thirty miles from Kuala Lumpur. Problems of establishing political control over the new colonial territory, while in some cases leading to a considerable influx of rural migrants into already existing centres, have led to the creation of many new settlements in Malaya. The contemporary hardening of the Cold War rivalries in Southeast Asia is also influencing the patterns of urbanization, particularly in South Vietnam and Thailand. In South Vietnam the construction of a series of seaports and military bases, intended as bastions from which the Americans will defend Vietnam, is completely altering the urban pattern. In Thailand the proliferation of American bases located mainly near provincial towns has given many of these quiet centres a boost for their economy.

The creation of a network of specialized industrial centres is just beginning in the majority of Southeast Asian countries, and certainly it has not yet eroded the dominance of the primate cities of Southeast Asia. In fact, with the exception of the socialist state of North Vietnam, most of the industrial development has been concentrated in the largest cities. For instance, one-third of all manufacturing establishments in the Philippines were concentrated in the Manila Metropolitan area in 1956. This figure had increased to 40 per cent by 1960. While the policy of establishing industrial estates adjacent to the major cities in Malaya has led to more industrial dispersion, Singapore has still continued to attract a large proportion of the industrial development. Unquestionably one of the main reasons for Singapore's breakaway from the Federation of Malaysia was the Central Government's plans to distribute industry more rationally which might have limited industrial development in Singapore. While Indonesia and Burma differ from the previous states in that there is more government control of economic development, they both have suffered from political instability in outlying areas which hindered programmes of regional industrial development, and confined it largely to the biggest cities. This is particularly well illustrated in the 1951 Industrialization Plan for Burma which intended to concentrate development in three main areas—first the area of Greater Rangoon, secondly the Myingyan area in the middle of the dry zone, and thirdly the Arakan area. In reality, political instability has forced most of the industrial development to be concentrated in the urban area of Rangoon, where a new cement factory, sawmill, textile factory and electrically operated steel mill have been established. In Indonesia where some urban-based industry had been developed under the Dutch during the 'thirties, the basic location of industry in towns such as Surabaja, has not been greatly changed.

Surprisingly, despite the fact that some industrial development has gone on in the 'great cities' of Southeast Asia, the proportions of the city labour force engaged in industrial occupations has not changed greatly from the colonial era. In some extreme cases the actual proportion employed in industry has declined, despite an increase in the industrial labour force. Thus in the case of Rangoon, Redick[15] records a decline in the percentage of the employed population in manufacturing from 24 per cent in 1931 to 18 per cent in 1953. This fall is explained partly by improved manufacturing techniques which reduce the labour need, and partly by the slowness in the pace of rebuilding manufacturing after the war, but principally by the considerable increase in the tertiary sector. In the same period the percentage of employed population in the tertiary sector (made up of commerce, transport and storage, construction, and government) inflated by the influx of rural refugees from the countryside, grew from 62·6 per cent to 79·0 per cent. This group moved, in particular, into the wholesale and retail sector, where the least skills and education were required. Similar patterns have been described for Djakarta.[16] The continuing dominance of the tertiary sector in the employment structure of the large Southeast Asian city is shown strikingly in the accompanying Table 6. Only Metropolitan Manila has more than 20 per cent of its population engaged in manufacturing activities, and in every one of these cities over two-thirds of the population

TABLE 6

PERCENTAGE OF LABOUR FORCE BY MAJOR INDUSTRIAL GROUP

For selected Southeast Asian cities

City	Agriculture Mining	Manufactur-ing	Construction	Commerce	Transport Storage Other Service	Govt. and Other Service	Not Adequately Described	Total
Met. Manila (1956)	2·8	21·3	6·4	19·2	9·4	39·0	1·9	100·0
Phnom-Penh (1959)	4·4	11·0	10·0	27·0	12·0	34·0	1·6	100·0
Met. Kuala Lumpur (1962)	3·0	17·0	5·0	25·0	10·0	40·0	—	100·0
Singapore Island (1957)	9·0	14·0	5·0	25·0	12·0	33·0	2·0	100·0
Bangkok (1960)	14·0	17·0	2·0	26·0	7·0	29·0	5·0	100·0
Djakarta Raya (1961)	5·0	16·0	9·0	24·0	13·0	33·0	—	100·0

Sources: Ramos (1961); Cambodian Census 1959 (1959); Department of Statistics, Federation of Malaya (1964); Chua (1964); Thailand Population Census 1960 (1961); Biro Pusat Statistik (1963).

Note: For Metropolitan Manila, Phnom Penh, Kuala Lumpur, Singapore Island and Djakarta Raya, the labour force is defined as those economically active over the age of 10. Bangkok's labour force is defined as those economically active over the age of 11.

was employed in tertiary activities. Within the tertiary sector commerce and government are the two largest employing groups. The concentration in government is hardly surprising since all these cities are political capitals. One of the consequences of independence has been a considerable growth in the number of civil servants as well as the armed forces and the police. Not only is the proportion employed in the tertiary sector high, but the cities also contain a high proportion of the specialized tertiary services of their respective countries. To take one extreme example from Thailand; in 1960 two-thirds of the country's physicians and surgeons were concentrated in the Bangkok metropolitan area which contained 8 per cent of the total population. As Ginsburg has pointed out, such concentration of services is a reflection of the basic rural structure of the Southeast Asian societies where there are '. . . only a limited number of services to be performed by cities. . . .'[17] It is significant that in countries with higher levels of urbanization, the services are less concentrated.

From the preceding section it is possible to conclude that while some industrial schemes have been started in the cities, they have not proved plentiful enough to provide adequate employment opportunities and the population has been forced into the already over-employed tertiary sector, or else are unemployed. Reliable data on the status of the unemployed in Southeast Asian cities, like so much other statistical information, is difficult to obtain and is further complicated by varying definitions of 'work force' and 'unemployment'. But enough information is on hand to indicate that serious unemployment problems exist in the majority of Southeast Asian cities; doubly severe, because unlike the Western cities, there are no well-established social welfare services operating. Thus, even in the capital cities of the Philippines and Malaysia, where there has been considerable construction and some manufacturing development, unemployment rates are high. For instance, 14·6 per cent of the males and 14·1 per cent of the females were unemployed in the Manila metropolitan area in 1956,[18] and 7·6 per cent of the males and 15 per cent of the females in Kuala Lumpur in 1962. The figures for Kuala Lumpur also

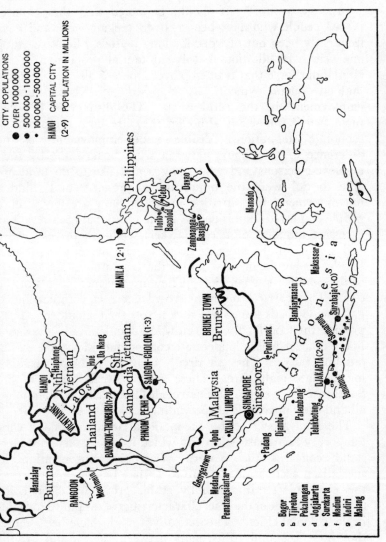

11 The Urban Pattern. Southeast Asia, 1960. Cities of 100,000 or more. Capitals and the major political divisions of the area.

show that unemployment is much greater in the younger age groups, rising to as high as 25 per cent for the males in the 15–19 age group.[19] It should be noted that these figures record people who have been actively seeking work and have frequently been out of work for long periods, often exceeding one year. In addition to this substantial proportion of the city labour force that is unemployed, there is also considerable 'hidden unemployment' as opposed to 'visible under-employment' in the rural areas. The distinction between these two is important although they are both symptoms of economic stagnation. 'Visible under-employment' is the difference in man hours between work being done by such employed persons and what they would like to do (and are able to do) were the opportunities present[20] and 'hidden unemployment' is a situation in which there are many more people employed than is necessary on a 'rational basis'.[21] The excessive numbers of street hawkers, pedi-cab drivers, office peons and family servants occurring in the city represents 'hidden unemployment'—one of the most ubiquitous features of the Southeast Asian city. They are the mendicants of the city. They carry through the crowded streets, with flat-footed gait, heavy loads slung on a stick across their shoulder. They provide the food for the overcrowded populations of the shop-house quarter where inadequate cooking facilities make eating out imperative. They sit tiredly on their pedi-cabs waiting for the late night fare. These are the 'real' people of the Southeast Asian city. Their struggle for a livelihood dominates all and their poverty is all-pervading.

The final aspect of the occupational structure of the contemporary Southeast Asian city which it is necessary to understand concerns the pattern of ethnic concentration in specialized occupational groups. It may be remembered that this economic stratification by ethnic group has been commented on as one of the chief characteristics of the plural societies in the colonial cities. Theoretically it might have been hoped that these economic differences between the various groups would begin to disappear with the growth of the independent city, particularly in view of the fact that political power has passed into the hands of the indigenes in virtually all cases.

The exception is Singapore. Certainly the proportion of alien Asian communities in the region has decreased, as is pointed out in a later section, but there is not the same degree of certainty that the occupational concentration of the various groups is breaking down. Economic measures against the Chinese in the Philippines and Indonesia may have reduced their concentration in commerce. Much more drastic measures in Burma against the Indians have led to their replacement by local people or state-controlled commercial establishments.

But the tendency described by Skinner for Bangkok,[22] where indigenous groups are 'polarized' at the extreme ends of the occupational scale from the government and the professions to the unskilled service and domestic occupations, while the alien Asian communities were concentrated in commercial, financial, industrial and artisan occupations, still occurs in many of the great cities of Southeast Asia. A glance at Table 7 which shows the employment patterns by industrial groups in two of the great cities of Southeast Asia (while they may not be regarded as altogether typical), indicates that the patterns of ethnic occupational concentration still persist, although in Rangoon, a sizeable influx of indigenous peoples, have begun to move into the commercial sector. Throughout the large cities of Southeast Asia today, the problem of occupational concentration poses a most severe difficulty to planning; the problem of how to integrate the indigenous groups into the wealthiest employment sector of the city—the commercial sector—and at the same time increase the participation of the alien groups in the political structure. The increasing drift to the city of the local people and their growing desire to enter urban occupations such as commerce and industry, at present monopolized by alien Asians, may well bring the problem of the plural societies to a head. In some cases this has already occurred. While much of the blame for the Singapore riots of 1964 between Chinese and Malays can be laid at the feet of the politicians, unquestionably the considerable discontent felt by the Singapore Malays at their failure to get jobs in the commercial sector, their lower levels of income, and higher rates of unemployment were important intensifying factors.[23] Whether

or not increased economic mobility and government inter-
ference can change this situation in the city is as yet not clear,
but for the moment the problem of the plural society in the
Southeast Asian city is one of the most crucial to be solved.

TABLE 7

PERCENTAGE OF LABOUR FORCE BY MAJOR INDUSTRIAL
GROUPS AND RACE FOR RANGOON AND PHNOM-PENH

RANGOON 1953
Racial Group

Industrial Group	Burmese	Other Indigenous	Chinese	Indian	Others	Total
Agriculture	1·1	0·9	1·2	1·3	—	1·1
Manufacturing	20·7	12·1	16·3	14·0	6·8	18·1
Construction	3·8	1·9	6·8	1·7	2·8	3·4
Commerce	31·0	36·9	53·0	41·4	33·0	38·0
Transport	14·2	13·6	5·2	7·6	17·9	11·9
Services	21·9	28·0	13·6	20·7	27·1	19·1
No adequate information	7·3	6·6	3·9	13·3	12·4	8·4
TOTAL	100·0	100·0	100·0	100·0	100·0	100·0

PHNOM-PENH 1959
Ethnic Group

Industrial Group	Cambodians	Vietnamese	Chinese	Others	Total
Agriculture	5·0	5·0	1·0	11·0	4·0
Manufacturing	8·0	16·0	15·0	13·0	11·0
Construction	7·0	17·0	2·0	5·0	10·0
Commerce	23·0	27·0	54·0	35·0	27·0
Transport, Electricity, etc.	14·0	10·0	3·0	3·0	12·0
Other Services	43·0	25·0	23·0	29·0	34·0
Not adequately described	—	—	2·0	4·0	2·0
TOTAL	100·0	100·0	100·0	100·0	100·0

Source: Redick (1961); Cambodian Census 1959 (1959).

THE SOCIAL STRUCTURE
OF THE SOUTHEAST ASIAN CITY

The hierarchical political and social structure of the colonial city, which segregated the various ethnic groups socially and ecologically, severely limited the possibility of social and economic mobility. The most clearly defined social group was the European *élite* who, together with the traditional indigenous aristocracy and a few of the wealthiest Asian entrepreneurs, formed the upper class. The middle class was made up of alien Asians, generally Chinese, who occupied positions in commerce, business and industry. Unskilled labourers, hawkers, and service workers of all kinds made up the lower classes and in this group there was a dominance of alien Asians, with a sprinkling of indigenous people. Theoretically, independence should create a situation in which this rigid social stratification of the city will be destroyed allowing a more flexible social structure to come into existence, bringing about greater mobility and mixing of the various ethnic groups.

Unquestionably the most radical change in the social structure has resulted from the transfer of European political power to the indigenous *élites* of these societies. In the place of the European *élites* of the colonial city, an increasingly augmented *élite* of indigenous aristocracy, government bureaucrats, military and political leaders and business entrepreneurs form the peak of the social structure. Members of this *élite* group, while voicing the need for traditional cultural values in the society, are frequently the most Westernized. Their homes are spacious, on Western lines; the symbols of status are the large American car and Western education. This upper class earns a high proportion of the city's income. In the Manila Metropolitan area for instance, 35·7 per cent of the total family income was earned by 8·7 per cent of the households.[24] Their conversation centres primarily on means of increasing their own wealth, the best universities overseas for their children's education and their overseas travel. Only occasionally do they seem to discuss their country's problems.

95

Mochtar Lubis, the Indonesian novelist, sums up the characteristics of these urban *élites*, in his character of Raden Kaslan—
the commercial importer oiling the party machine to ensure
his profits. Lubis leaves little doubt concerning his feelings
on the role of such groups in the new society, and the manner
in which their wealth is spent '. . . Raden Kaslan was at the
wheel, and at his side sat his wife Fatma. From the dark-red
Cadillac, up to Fatma's finery, her elaborate gold slippers, her
coiffure fresh from the hairdresser's salon, emanated an air of
luxury and wealth'.[25] It would appear that in many ways the
new *élite* are as far from understanding the problems of housing,
employment and health which concern the great mass of the
city dwellers, as were the colonial *élites*. In addition to this
élite social group there is also a growing upper middle class
made up of office and bank workers, less senior government
officials, and university and secondary school teachers. A
growing intelligentsia and the large numbers of journalists who
concentrate in the capital city are also drawn from this class.
While the Western symbols of status are less common in this
group, most of them desire to imitate the pattern of the *élites*
who in turn model their behaviour on the ways of the West.[26]

Beneath this Westernized *élite* and upper middle class are
the commercial middle classes earlier discussed, and finally
there are the working-class groups—factory workers, petty
traders, the betja riders (trishaw cyclists) and itinerant hawkers
who make up by far the largest proportion of the city population. Frequently, this latter group is made up of the most
recent migrants who lack the basic educational skills to enable
them to find permanent employment in the city. What jobs
they can find are only short-term labouring jobs and the
unemployment rates are highest amongst this group. This
poor working class is forced into the proliferating squatter
settlements on the fringes of the city because they do not have
the income to afford better housing. These recent migrants
come to the city in search of a better income and livelihood
but frequently find nothing but poverty; their upward mobility
is blocked by their lack of skills and the persistence of the
ethnic monopoly of many jobs—all of which adds up to a
situation in which the social structure in many ways is no less

1. Rural Idyll. Malay rural housing in Kelantan on the east coast of the Malayan Peninsula.

URBAN-RURAL CONTRASTS

2. Urban Squalor. Squatter housing on the fringes of Singapore city. These squatters are more fortunate than most for at least they have piped water and tin roofs.

3. Rural Toil.   Malay peasants ploughing ricefields prior to planting, Province Wellesley, Malaysia.

URBAN-RURAL CONTRASTS

4. Urban Ease.   Luxurious housing in the new *élite* housing of Kenny Hill, Kuala Lumpur.

5. Rural Isolation. A Chinese fishing village on the west coast of peninsular Malaysia. Its only contact with urban centres is by boat.

URBAN-RURAL CONTRASTS

6. Urban Contact. The overcrowded tenement slums of Singapore city.
(D. W. McKenzie)

7. Angkor Vat is a replica in stone of the Khmer cosmology.   The five towers symbolize Meru's five peaks, the enclosing wall represents the mountains at the edge of the world, and the surrounding moat the ocean beyond.   (*Keith Buchanan*)

THE PRE-INDUSTRIAL CITY

8. One of the five towered entrances to Angkor Thom. A naga balustrade is supported by figures of good spirits. *(Keith Buchanan)*

THE PRE-INDUSTRIAL CITY

9. The royal palace compound in Phnom-Penh city. The Mekong is in the background. Phnom-Penh is one of the few Southeast Asian pre-industrial cities which has remained the capital of a new nation. (*Geographical Handbook Series*)

THE PRE-INDUSTRIAL CITY

10. Thanh Hoa. An Annamite citadel town with buildings of the indigenous population clustered round it. *(Geographical Handbook Series)*

THE PRE-INDUSTRIAL CITY

11. A seventeenth-century sketch of Mrauk-u from the Portuguese quarter of Daingri-pet. *(Schouten, 1676)*

INDIGENOUS CITY AND COLONIAL STABILIZING POINT

12. Portuguese Malacca, showing the walls of the fort and the main buildings. (Compare Figure 5). *(Survey Department, Federation of Malaysia)*

13. A contemporary view of the Dutch Stadt Huis built after their occupation of Malacca in 1641. It still serves as State Government offices.

THE COLONIAL CITY—PEAK AND DECLINE

14. The Port of Malacca. Now sadly declined from its years of greatness under the Malacca Sultanate, the Portuguese and the Dutch.

15. Chinese street in Batavia in the nineteenth century. The appearance of these areas has changed little. In the foreground runs one of the many canals which were important transport routes in the city. *(Koninklijk Institout Voor de Tropen)*

ETHNIC QUARTERS IN THE COLONIAL CITY

16. A former French quarter of Hanoi. This recent picture indicates few changes in the physical appearance of the housing. The city has, however, undergone radical changes in its economic structure. *(Keith Buchanan)*

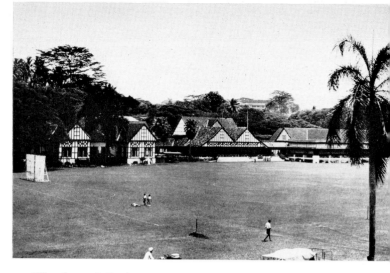

17. 'The Spotted Dog'. The Selangor Club which was the chief social centre of the European community in the colonial days of Kuala Lumpur. Today it is a multi-racial club for the city's new *élites*.

THE 'EUROPEAN' COLONIAL CITY

18. A typical European colonial house. Note the elevated position of the house and the verandahs which surround it ensuring a maximum coolness.

19. The 'Grafted Colonial Town'. An aerial view of Rangoon with the Shwe Dagon pagoda in the foreground. Surrounding it is the fossil area of high-class housing, formerly occupied by Europeans.

TYPES OF COLONIAL TOWN

20. The 'Planned Colonial City'. Present-day Singapore, looking across the roofs of Chinatown to the Singapore river and the zone of mercantile and government buildings. The numerous sampans on the river are unloading goods from the outer harbour. (*K. Buchanan*)

21. A street scene in Kuala Lumpur. China-towns form the core of most of the Southeast Asian cities. While the commercial activities of the Chinese focuses on the front of the shop-house much of the household activity is carried in the back streets.

THE ECOLOGICAL AREAS OF THE SOUTHEAST ASIAN CITY

22. In many of the cities new residential quarters are growing rapidly. This illustration shows a new block of flats in Phnom-Penh. In the background is the traditional architecture of a Buddhist temple.
(*Keith Buchanan*)

23. The growth of air travel has rapidly brought the great cities of Southeast Asia into the network of international tourism. While cities such as Bangkok and Singapore have been the main centres of tourism, even the smaller centres have built high-class hotels to attract tourists. The Lane Xang Hotel in Vientiane cost over one million U.S. dollars to build.   (*Keith Buchanan*)

THE CHANGING FACE OF THE SOUTHEAST ASIAN CITY

24. Bangkok is justly called the 'Venice of the East'. But recently many canals have been filled in and used as roads.

25. One of the principal means of transport in the city is the human-powered trishaw. This illustration shows a trishaw driver outside the main market in Kuala Lumpur.

TRANSPORT IN THE SOUTHEAST ASIAN CITY

26. But increasingly the human-powered trishaws are being replaced by motorized transport. In Bangkok they have been replaced entirely by motorized trishaws such as this one.

(*D. W. McKenzie*)

27. The bicycle remains one of the most important forms of transport. A street scene in Saigon, showing three immaculately dressed female cyclists in the bustle of one of the main streets. (*D. W. McKenzie*)

TRANSPORT IN THE SOUTHEAST ASIAN CITY

28. Human labour and human transport are still significant in shifting goods. This picture shows a street hawker in Bangkok with his goods in baskets on the ends of a carrying-pole. (*D. W. McKenzie*)

29. Street markets and street hawkers form an ubiquitous feature of retailing practice of the Southeast Asian city. Here women are selling fruit on Saigon streets.

(D. W. McKenzie)

THE MARKETS OF THE SOUTHEAST ASIAN CITY

30. All the large Southeast Asian cities have central markets where the majority of foodstuffs for the city is sold. The main market in Kuala Lumpur.

31. Cottage industry is still the major type of industry in most Southeast Asian cities. Often the numerous small-scale industries, such as the car repair industry in Kuala Lumpur, sprawl along the main entrances to the city, adding to the traffic congestion.

INDUSTRY IN THE SOUTHEAST ASIAN CITY

32. Larger scale industry, using mechanical power and concentrated in industrial estates on the fringes of the city, is growing. A Pepsi-Cola factory in the new industrial estate of Petaling Jaya, five miles outside Kuala Lumpur.

33. The Western commercial district is characterized by the prevalence of European-owned banks. The Chartered Bank in Kuala Lumpur.

COMMERCE IN THE SOUTHEAST ASIAN CITY

34. The indigenous systems of credit. Chettyar money-lenders, Ampang Street, Kuala Lumpur.

35. A new element of the 'westernized commercial district'. The car-retailing zone in Bangkok.

SPECIALIZED 'WESTERNIZED ZONES' IN THE SOUTHEAST ASIAN CITY

36. The 'Western' entertainment quarter is located close to the Western commercial zone in most Southeast Asian cities. The 'western' entertainment area of Phnom-Penh. French-style restaurants are also located in the same area. (*Keith Buchanan*)

37. The 'western' shopping district in Phnom-Penh. The French influence still remains in the tree-lined streets and the awnings outside the shops. (*Keith Buchanan*)

WESTERN INFLUENCES IN THE SOUTHEAST ASIAN CITY

38. New middle-class suburbs. Government housing in Djakarta. (*Camera Press*)

39. Housing built on the marshy land adjacent to the river, on the urban fringes of Phnom-Penh. Rural housing characteristically built on stilts is well designed for such an environment.   (*Keith Buchanan*)

'*AQUATIC*' *SUBURBS IN THE SOUTHEAST ASIAN CITY*

40. Housing lining the *klongs* (canals) of Bangkok is even more orientated to an aquatic environment. The *klongs* are the main streets, and boats a universal form of transport.

'AQUATIC' SUBURBS IN THE SOUTHEAST ASIAN CITY

41. The 'Americanization' of Manila. The supermarket and the sales shop for the suburban bungalows of the growing middle classes of Manila city. *(Camera Press)*

THE MAIN ECOLOGICAL ZONES OF MANILA CITY

42. The fringes of Binondo District. The architectural styles of the 'western commercial district' are already beginning to intrude. In the background the dome of the Catholic church looms against the sky.

43. Kuala Lumpur's Chinatown. The bottom half of the buildings are given over to commerce. The second storey is made up of large rooms subdivided into many cubicles, in which people live. The central shop shown here is a Chinese funeral shop with paper figures of animals.

RESIDENTIAL AREAS OF KUALA LUMPUR

44. Malay housing in Kampong Bharu. A residential area reserved for Malays of Kuala Lumpur. It has recently become grossly over-crowded and many Malays have been forced into squatter areas. The persistence of rural housing styles is marked. (Compare with Plate 1.)

45. An aerial view of Petaling Jaya which indicates the visual similarities with the suburbs of Western cities. The prevalence of the bungalow and the residential section is most clearly marked.

RESIDENTIAL AREAS IN KUALA LUMPUR

46. One of the Petaling Jaya shopping centres which are modelled on those of the New Towns in the United Kingdom.

47. Inner core squatters living in cramped conditions in the Intramuros area of Manila city. Their houses are built of makeshift
materials, and there are inadequate sanitary, power and water
facilities.

SQUATTERS IN THE SOUTHEAST ASIAN CITY

48. Outer fringe squatters in Quezon city on the outskirts of Manila.
Here there is ample space for gardens which provide food to supplement
what is often an inadequate income.

49. Congested squatter housing in Singapore city.

SQUATTERS IN THE SOUTHEAST ASIAN CITY

50. 'Aquatic' squatters. A village of illegal housing built on piles over the Rochore River, close to the city of Singapore.

51. A 'high-rise' housing development to the south of the Gombak River. (See Figure 35.) These flats were originally built to house resettled squatters, but many have since moved out. (*D. W. McKenzie*)

RESETTLEMENT—THE SOLUTION OF THE SQUATTER PROBLEM?

52. An aerial view of new housing developments in Singapore, which shows the careful provision of schools and other facilities. But can the provision of housing keep pace with the rapid growth of population? (*D. W. McKenzie*)

53. Food for the city. A heavily laden boat bringing produce down the Chao Phraya River to feed Bangkok. Caught in the vicious cycle of increasing population and economic under-development, can the countryside continue to provide the city with food without starving itself?

THE FUTURE OF THE SOUTHEAST ASIAN CITY

54. The new educational institutions for training the cadres of the new nations are almost entirely urban-based. A new university in Phnom-Penh, financed in part by Russian aid. (*Keith Buchanan*)

55. The ethnic complexity of the Southeast Asian city. This parking sign, in a Singapore street, written in four languages, demonstrates the multi-racial character of the city.   Can these ethnic differences be merged into a common nationhood in the melting pot of the city?

(*D. W. McKenzie*)

THE FUTURE OF THE SOUTHEAST ASIAN CITY

56. The angry people of the city.   Rioters in Djakarta.   Who will decide the future
of the Southeast Asian city?   The angry people of the city or the well-fed *élites*?
(Associated Press)

THE FUTURE OF THE SOUTHEAST ASIAN CITY

rigid than that of the colonial era, despite the growth of the urban *élites* and the upper middle class.

Theoretically, changes in a city's population composition should encourage changes in the social structure. In virtually all the large Southeast Asian cities the proportion of aliens has declined. In some instances this reflects the increasing movement to the city of indigenes rather than the numerical decline of the alien groups. In Djakarta, for instance, the number of Chinese has increased from 76,000 in 1930 to 280,000 in 1957, while their proportion has decreased from 14 per cent to 10 per cent. In other cities there has been a decline in the number of aliens. Thus in Rangoon in 1953 the number of Indians had fallen below their prewar figure. In such circumstances the possibilities for the indigenous people to break into the commercial and business occupations, and to gain upward social mobility are considerably enhanced, although even then their lack of training and entrepreneurial skills often means that the government must take over certain of the activities in this sector. In some countries where measures against the Chinese have been less repressive, the government is attempting to integrate the indigenous groups into the commercial sector by issuing new retailing and manufacturing licences to indigenes and by providing substantial government capital to encourage indigenous industry. In Malaysia, for instance, the government has been devoting a considerable amount of energy to the task of directing the indigenous Malay into commercial and industrial activity, but as yet have had limited success. But overall, despite the numerical growth of indigenes, the middle classes of the Asian city are still dominated by the 'alien' Asian groups, and mobility into this sector is exceptionally difficult.

These conclusions, while admittedly based largely on a subjective assessment, do raise the important question of whether or not urban centres in Southeast Asia provide the type of environment in which social change is occurring at a rapid rate. Few writers have contested the view that the transition from rural to urban life in the Western world involved fundamental changes in the organization of society, the social relations of the individual and his personality, but considerable doubts have been expressed by workers in the non-Western city that similar patterns of social change are occurring. For instance, Edward Bruner's research into the patterns of urbanization amongst the Toba Batak living in the city of Medan in North Sumatra leads him to the conclusion that, 'It is clear that the social concomitants of the transition from rural to urban life are not the same in Southeast Asia as in Western society.'[27] Hauser has summarized the reasons in the following passage:

> Although the large cities in Asia have great size, their pluralistic composition and characteristic dual economies have enabled indigenous groups to live under essentially 'folk' conditions within the boundaries of the city. Despite their relatively high densities, life has not necessarily become largely secularized, great differentiation of functions has not taken place and the way of life has not changed markedly for many of the indigenous population groups. Finally despite the great heterogeneity of the population in many of these cities, both exogenous and indigenous ethnic groups, little has occurred in the way of increased sophistication, rationality in behaviour, cosmopolitanism of outlook or innovation and social change. In large measure, the problems—social and personal—in the great cities of Asia, derive not so much from 'urbanism as a way of life' but reflect rather the problems of the nation at large, problems arising largely from low productivity and mass poverty.[28]

The assumption implicit in this statement is that social change is not occurring because there is little evidence that an 'urban way of life' similar to the West is emerging except amongst a small urban *élite* and upper middle class. While one may be critical of the assumption that social change must involve some move towards a universal Western pattern, one cannot deny that the influx of people into the great cities has retarded the progress of social change. Lucien Pye has shown how the flood of refugees into Rangoon '. . . began to outstrip the pace at which the appropriate modern forms of social control could be introduced; hence there was a tendency to revert to more traditional forms of social control'.[29] The shortage of housing forced the in-migrants into squatter

colonies or *Kwetthits*, each of which was placed under the
control of a headman who was responsible for its inhabitants
to the city authorities. Rangoon city has become a collection
of village communities in which 'face to face relationships'
have become all important and community ties are reinforced.[30]
A similar intensification of community attitudes seems to be
occurring with the increasing movement of Malays into the
hitherto Chinese-dominated cities of Malaya.[31]

Clearly it is too easy to argue that the colonial phase of
Southeast Asian city growth, when the cities were peopled by
alien ethnic groups, is finished because the cities are no longer
growing from outside immigration. It would appear that the
pluralistic nature of indigenous society in Southeast Asia
accounts for the peopling of the contemporary cities by almost
as great a diversity of peoples. As Bruner comments,

> Every national Medan is, of course an Indonesian citizen,
> but in terms of the language he speaks at home, the cultural
> tradition he follows, and the social group of which he is
> part, he is also a Javanese, a Malay, an Atjehnese, a
> Minangkabau, a Mandailing, an Angkola, a Simelungun,
> a Karo, a Pak-Pak, or something else. Medan consists
> of a series of separate ethnic communities as well as social
> enclaves of Chinese, Indians and Europeans.[32]

The implications are that the current phase of city growth will
see the persistence of the plural societies in the great cities,
which in turn will prevent the integrations of minds and
societies which are so necessary for the emergence of a national
culture.

Needless to say, this rapid influx of populations has posed
severe problems to city government and planning. Under the
demographic, social and economic pressures which have
emerged in the postwar Southeast Asian city, few elective city
governments have been able to operate. Only in the Philippines, Malaysia, and Singapore have the city governments
continued to be elected. In most cases the city government
has become part of the national administration, and authoritarian city rule has been necessary to cope with the problems
of the city.[33]

99

The persistence of the complex social, ethnic and economic divisions of the city conflicts with the cultural role the great cities must play in the newly independent nations as the centres of, and disseminating points for, the new national cultures. It is surely paradoxical that in a city such as Kuala Lumpur, the capital of the Federation of Malaysia, and the centre from which the urban *élites* disseminate the elements of a new Malayan culture which attempts to integrate the diverse ethnic elements and cultures into a common Malayan culture, is still characterized by the very divisions in the society which it is trying to wield together.[34] It is logical to assume that with independence, these colonial cities tainted with the stigma of colonialism would have proved unsuitable in the eyes of the new national leaders to be used as capitals. But while suggestions were put forward to build new capitals on the sites of the older pre-industrial capitals, where they would be untainted with colonialism, only in one country was a new capital built. The exception was in the Philippines where a new capital, Quezon city, was located, not on a pre-industrial site, but close to the old capital of colonial times, Manila city. The break-up of some of the larger colonial units, particularly French Indochina, has caused the upgrading of former colonial provincial towns to the status of capitals, notably in the case of Kuala Lumpur and Phnom-Penh. But as Rhoads Murphey comments, the overwhelming advantages of the colonial capitals as centres of the transportation network and commerce and administration have discouraged any relocation of the capitals.[35]

Thus it is from the base of the former colonial cities, now the independent capitals, that the urban-based *élites* are attempting to accomplish the difficult task of building a sense of common nationality in their countries' population. The Southeast Asian capitals have now assumed in Redfield and Singer's terminology an 'orthogenetic' role, in which the city's role is to put forward the image of a national culture which in many of these countries barely exists. It is not surprising, therefore, that the city is the centre of the institutions which are expected to disseminate the ideas of the new culture. Universities, training colleges, language schools, military institutes, cultural and political institutions are largely located in the capital city. The national leadership of the country is concentrated here, where they have '. . . greater access to the central government organs, the largest business firms, the best educational institutions and the national mass media'.[36] The encadrement of the teachers of the new ethos is carried out by bringing the potential cadres to the city, training them there, and then encouraging them to return to the countryside imbued with new skills and a commitment to spread ideals of the new nation throughout the country. Too often, however, the well-trained technicians, teachers and doctors, cannot be convinced of the necessity to return to the rural countryside where their skills are needed. Of course, if they are employed by the government they must go where they are appointed, but eventually they will work their way back to the city. To take one example, which is repeated on a smaller scale in many other countries in Southeast Asia, 78 per cent of all Thailand's university graduates were concentrated in the Bangkok–Thonburi metropolitan area which contained just 8 per cent of the total population in 1960. This gross imbalance in the distribution of the individuals who, it might be claimed, are most likely to 'spark' change in their countries, poses severe problems in the task of nation-state building in which the cities play such a central role.

In effect the whole process of encadrement in the cities is self-defeating, for this type of nationalism is essentially an urban-based phenomenon which involves education in Western values. But the moment the potential cadre becomes educated in the Western patterns, he begins to be separated from the traditional values of the countryside, and attracted by the superficial Westernization of the city. The cities are the centre of the auditory and visual communications media, much of which comes from the West. The cities offer entertainment, higher incomes and the specialized services which can be obtained nowhere else in the country. The cities are also the headquarters for the major political parties and cliques of the country and draw much of their support from the urban-based businessmen, the army, and only too often the interfering foreign power. It is natural, therefore, for the enterprising

educated to stay in the city to seek their way to the top.
Frequently they end up as in this description of Bangkok,
'At night, as the lights of thousands of coloured neon signs
illuminate the city's bars and bath houses, the pampered youth
of Thailand's jet set speed up in flashy sports cars to chic Pat
Pong Road where they while away the evening in luxurious
night clubs.'[37]   Or like this,

> There is still much that is rotten in the heart of South
> Vietnamese society. While many able men serve the
> government with dedication, corruption has been only
> partly checked, and night clubs in the capital are filled
> with elegant young men, twisting and sipping champagne,
> who have bought their way out of the military service.[38]

In overall terms we can see the end product of this kind of
development in South Vietnam, where the increasing social
and economic imbalance between countryside and city is
leading inevitably to the alienation of the peasants and to the
physical loss of control of the countryside.   The city increasingly takes on the hue of the pre-industrial city, but now instead
of court cliques, it is the military, political and foreign-
supported factions who fight to decide who is to control the city.
The cities become more and more isolated from the countryside, relying on foreign aid for their continued existence.   The
economies of the cities are undermined by inflation.   Thus in
1965 food prices in Saigon rose by 50 per cent '. . . and many
people have trouble affording such basic commodities as cloth
and charcoal'.[39]   Can the 'elegant young men' of Southeast
Asia's cities solve their countries' problems?
   The preceding discussion has dealt in very general terms with
the systematic elements of the contemporary Southeast Asian
city.   Varying rates of economic growth, and degrees of
political stability and national integration have further complicated the task of building up a comprehensive picture of the
pattern of urbanization.   Nevertheless, a preliminary classification of the network of urban centres in Southeast Asia can be
attempted by slightly modifying a classification of cities
attempted by Hildred Geertz on the basis of the cities'.
'structural relationships . . . with the nation . . . and the

external world'.[40] On such a basis she suggests a twofold
division of the cities of Indonesia into 'metropoles' and 'provincial towns'. In the context of Southeast Asia the sub-
division of true metropoles from the 'emerging metropoles'
allows the introduction of some of the smaller capitals such as
Kuala Lumpur and Phnom-Penh; in addition a new category
is made for the specialized single function towns such as the
oil-producing town of Seria in Brunei.

The 'metropoles' of Southeast Asia are the great cities of
Southeast Asia—Djakarta, Bangkok, Rangoon, Manila, Singapore and Saigon-Cholon. They serve both as connecting links
with other nations and as integrating centres of economic,
political and intellectual life. In them are located the out-
posts of Western finance, the diplomatic corps, the highest
administrative and legislative organs of the national government, the central offices of the political organizations, the main
industry and commercial organizations, the main universities
and the offices and publication centres of the main newspapers.
Socially these cities are characterized by extremely mixed and
heterogeneous communities which, while they have ample contact, tend to remain in largely 'encapsulated communities'.
There are large communities of foreign merchants—Chinese,
Indians, and so forth who still form an important proportion
of the population. The indigenous community generally
occupies the peak of the social pyramid and the lowest echelons.
The middle class consists largely of aliens, although in Indonesia and the Philippines the indigenous people are increasingly
moving into this group. The 'metropoles' have a dispropor-
tionate share of the services of the country, particularly the
communications media, the medical and educational services.
The 'metropoles' of Southeast Asia are largely distinguished by
the fact that they form part of what may be called the metropolitan 'super-culture' of the world.

The 'emerging metropoles', such as Kuala Lumpur and
Phnom-Penh, share practically all the features of the metropoles
with the exception of size. Their chief characteristic has been
the exceptionally rapid growth of their populations since
independence along with the growth of government and
commerce in the new centres. There is some argument for

including some of the largest regional capitals in this category for they too have close contact with other nations. For instance, the regional capital of Medan in Sumatra increased its population by over 500 per cent between 1930 and 1961, an increase even higher than Djakarta, while at the same time gaining greatly in importance as a regional administrative and trading centre. By 1959 there were three universities, three additional institutions of higher learning, over 200 elementary schools, and eleven consulates and trade representatives in the city and by practically every criterion the centre deserves to be labelled an 'emerging metropole'.[41]

Thirdly, there are the provincial towns. While it is difficult to categorize some of the more rapidly growing provincial towns (Cebu, the second largest city in the Philippines is a good example of this problem),[42] the provincial town is generally distinguished from the metropole by its smaller population, its outlying location, and its closer links with its hinterland. The population of these towns is more stable than in the 'metropoles'. They have fewer Westerners and aliens and generally city life revolves around the '. . . two main institutional complexes, government and trade'.[43] The government employees in the town are divided into two broad groups: (a) national civil servants who may have been transferred from the centre to the periphery to establish and continue contacts with the central government, and (b) the locally-appointed civil servants who most frequently occupy the lower rungs of the civil service ladder and do not move from the town. Trade and commerce are still dominated by local groups. The mass of the population is poorly educated and unskilled. Hubert Freyn has described some of these aspects in his description of Nakorn Sritamaraj, a small provincial town in the south of Thailand, commenting on the '. . . ever-changing Bangkok-appointed official hierarchy, from the Governor down to the teachers in the Government schools'.[44] From a national point of view these provincial towns play their most important role as sub-disseminating centres of the national ethos. The relationship between the provincial towns and the surrounding countryside is a fascinating and important aspect of the role of the provincial cities which as yet has been little investigated. Donn Hart has shown the central role which the Philippine plaza complex plays as the focus of the activities of the town and its rural hinterland. The rural folk from the surrounding barrios (rural districts) come to the town for their administrative contacts with the central government, to sell their goods at the market-place on the weekly market day, and to take part in the many religious and national festivals and celebrations. The provincial town becomes a mixing place for the rural and urban folk and even although, as Hart comments 'tempered by social distance', this mixing must 'result in the exchange of new ideas and attitudes'.[45] The provincial town is also the disseminating centre of national information and new innovations. Thus the provincial cities play a vital role in the urban network.

Finally, there are the single function urban centres of which the mineral exploitation towns are the best example. Their characteristics are much the same throughout the world; they have a transient air which reflects the inevitable depletion of the resources which they are exploiting. In Southeast Asia these mineral exploiting towns are often isolated from the surrounding urban network, linked only to the port where the minerals are exported. They often have large communities of European technicians and managers who live in encapsulated communities completely separate from the country. The labour is most frequently alien Asian, although in such countries as Malaysia and Brunei an increasing amount of indigenous labour is being employed and trained. Often the towns are physically separated from the surrounding areas by fences and 'keep out' notices, as if in the age of nationalism the foreign-administered mining towns are on the defensive and are protecting themselves against the encroachment of local interest.

It is clear from this account that it is the 'metropoles' which still dominate the urban hierarchy. It is obvious, too, that the character and role of these 'metropoles' are greatly influencing the manner in which many of the Southeast Asian societies are developing. The remaining chapters treat in greater detail some of the demographic, social and economic aspects of these great cities of Southeast Asia.

CHAPTER 6

The Demographic Character of the Southeast Asian City

A RECURRENT THEME running through sociological literature on the non-Western city is the comparison of its demographic and ecological characteristics with the urban patterns of Western industrialized nations. This and the ensuing chapters are no exception to this general rule in that they attempt to show in what way some of the great cities of Southeast Asia diverge from the Western cities, in order to establish some of the unique aspects of the Southeast Asian city. While it is obvious that the cultural, historical and institutional differences amongst Western societies do cause some variation in the demographic character of these Western cities,[1] fairly universal agreement has been reached about the following generalizations:

  (i) a tendency for an urban centre of high density to be surrounded by rings of lower population density;
  (ii) the spatial growth of the city to be largely centrifugal with the outer areas of the city growing at faster rates than the inner core;
  (iii) the pattern of urban population increase is both age and sex selective, characterized by a concentration in the age group between 15–60, and by a dominance of females as compared to the total population;
  (iv) within the city itself the pattern of age concentration in the age group 15–60 decreases as the population spreads out from the city core, while the masculinity of the population increases towards the city core;
  (v) during the periods of most rapid growth a large proportion of the urban population increase is made up of in-migration; and finally

(vi) the urban way of life tends to have certain disruptive effects on the traditional patterns of family life.

The lack of overall data for all the large Southeast Asian cities makes comparison difficult, but enough data is at hand to suggest that there is substantial variation not only from the

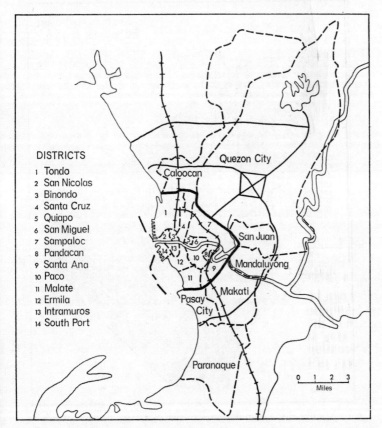

DISTRICTS
1 Tondo
2 San Nicolas
3 Binondo
4 Santa Cruz
5 Quiapo
6 San Miguel
7 Sampaloc
8 Pandacan
9 Santa Ana
10 Paco
11 Malate
12 Ermita
13 Intramuros
14 South Port

12 Manila Metropolitan area. Reference map showing major census districts of Manila city and adjacent urban areas.

Western model but amongst the various Southeast Asian cities as well.

First, it is clear that the majority of the large Southeast Asian cities have experienced patterns of centrifugal city expansion similar to that of Western cities. The accompanying Table 8 and maps of selected Southeast Asian cities illustrates that with few exceptions, the outer areas have been growing much more rapidly than the inner-city core. The growth of the inner district of Intramuros (Ward 13, Figures 12 and 13), Manila

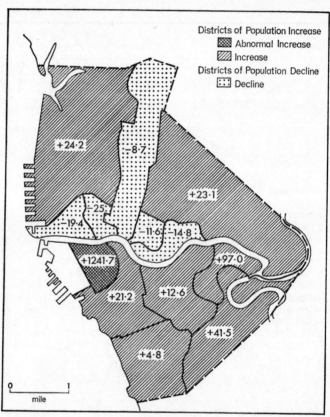

13 Manila city. Population increase by census districts, 1948–60.

city can be regarded as abnormal. In fact, this district, which encompasses the old Spanish fort and original pre-industrial core of the city, experienced an influx of illegal squatters into the area after it had been badly bombed during the Japanese occupation, increasing the population from 987 in 1948 to 13,243 in 1960. What is not so clear, however, are the forces bringing about this pattern of centrifugal expansion. In the Western cities this spatial growth was associated with the development of rapid transit facilities and the widespread use of the automobile which brought about residential deconcentration, and the almost complete separation of place of residence

TABLE 8

PERCENTAGE POPULATION CHANGE BY INNER AND OUTER ZONES FOR SELECTED SOUTHEAST ASIAN CITIES

Rangoon	Inner Core	Transitional Zone	Outer Zone
1921–1931	+ 3·9	+20·8	+ 23·7
1931–1953	+19·9	+94·2	+ 129·8
Manila	Inner Core	Outer Zone	
1918–1939	+61·7	+ 148·2	
1939–1948	+13·1	+ 66·5	
1948–1960	− 11·9	+ 30·8	
Singapore			
1947–1957	+28·4	+ 41·2	

Sources: Redick (1961); Philippines Census Report 1960, Summary Report (1963); Del Tufo (1949); Chua (1960).

TABLE 9

CHANGES IN DENSITY BY INNER AND OUTER ZONES FOR SELECTED SOUTHEAST ASIAN CITIES

DENSITY PER SQUARE MILE

Rangoon	Inner Core	Transitional Zone	Outer Zone
1921	115,000	20,000	6,000
1931	120,000	24,000	8,000
1953	144,000	47,000	18,000
Manila	Inner Core	Outer Zone	
1918	91,000	10,000	
1939	148,000	24,000	
1948	167,000	40,000	
Singapore			
1947	120,000	13,000	
1957	189,000	15,000	

Sources: Redick (1961); Philippines Census Report 1960, Summary Report (1963); Del Tufo (1949); Chua (1960).

and place of work. As shown in Table 9, which gives densities for selected Southeast Asian cities by inner and outer areas, both Rangoon and Singapore, despite the rapid growth of the outer areas, have not experienced a decline of the inner city densities. Manila, on the other hand, as Table 9 reveals, shows significant declines in the inner core populations. The

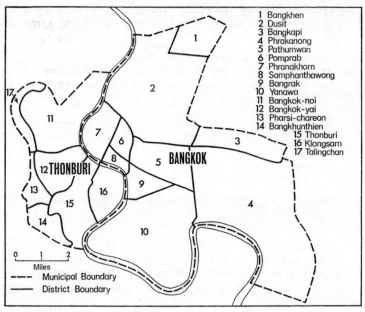

14   Bangkok Metropolitan area.   Reference map showing census districts, 1960.

distinction between Manila and the other cities is explained by the different circumstances of growth in the last twenty years. Rangoon and cities like it, such as Djakarta and Saigon-Cholon which have experienced a considerable influx of rural refugees since 1947, have not been able to absorb these populations (largely indigenous) within the inner parts of the city, already heavily populated by alien groups, and the rural migrants have been forced to the fringes of the city. Here they live in rural-like villages retaining the patterns of social organization and life which existed in their home villages.

This process has also been aided by the pressure that the influx of population has placed on the existing metropolitan transportation and housing which have become completely inadequate, discouraging any residential deconcentration except amongst the wealthy *élites*.[2] In Manila, while there has been a similar influx of population locating itself on the fringes of

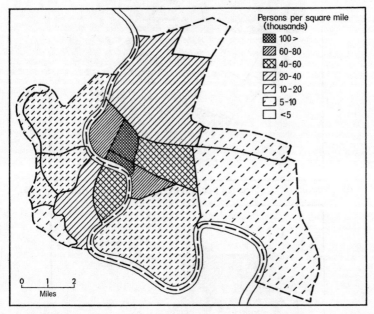

Persons per square mile
(thousands)

100 >
60-80
40-60
20-40
10-20
5-10
<5

0   1   2
Miles

15   Bangkok Metropolitan area. Density per square mile by census
     districts, 1960.

the city, the declining densities of the inner core suggest residential deconcentration and the growth of suburbs in the surrounding areas has been probably the most rapid of any Southeast Asian city.

In general, while the density patterns of the Southeast Asian cities show the same spatial pattern of declining densities away from the central core which characterizes the Western cities, they vary considerably from the Western pattern and amongst themselves with respect to a single urban centre of high population density (Figures 15 and 16). In part this is explained by

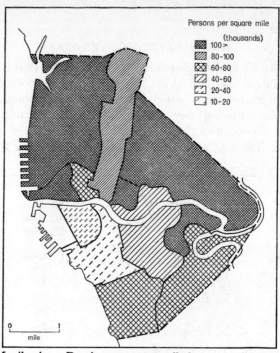

16 Manila city. Density per square mile by census districts, 1960.

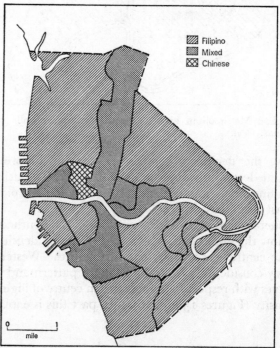

17 Manila city. Distribution of main ethnic groups by census districts,
    1960. The Filipino districts have more than 93 per cent of their
    population made up of Filipinos. The Chinese district more than
    66 per cent. The remaining districts have mixed populations of
    Filipinos, Chinese and Europeans.

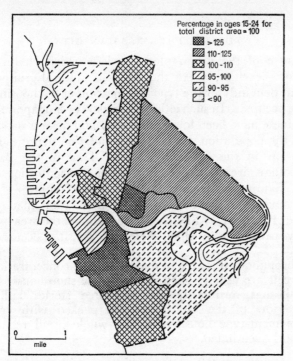

Percentage in ages 15-24 for
total district area = 100

- \> 125
- 110 - 125
- 100 - 110
- 95 - 100
- 90 - 95
- < 90

0   1
mile

18 Manila city. Concentration in ages 15–24, 1960.

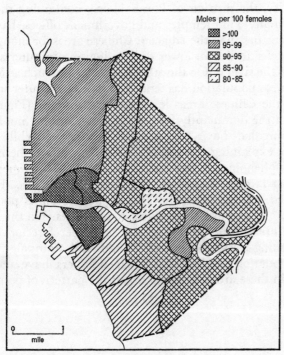

Males per 100 females

- \> 100
- 95 - 99
- 90 - 95
- 85 - 90
- 80 - 85

0   1
mile

19 Manila city. Sex ratios by census districts, 1960.

the nature of the urban plural society which characterizes many of the cities, where the different cultural groups have different demands for the type and location of the housing they want to occupy. In such cities as Bangkok or Singapore, where the Chinese have been long established and form a substantial part of the population, the highest population densities invariably occur in the Chinese quarter. Thus in the Bangkok metropolitan area the main population concentration occurs in the Samphanthawong, Bangrak and Pomprab districts which have over two-thirds of their population made up of Chinese (Figure 21). Skinner's description of the area explains the physical milieu in which these high densities occur:

> Throughout this area of major Chinese concentration, the streets are usually lined with Chinese shop-houses in row buildings, ordinarily two to three stories tall. The interiors of the big blocks are packed with crowded tenement-type housing, on the whole in ill repair and poorly ventilated.[3]

The Chinese pattern of combining residence with place of work also accounts for these high densities. The true core of the city, the districts of Phranakhorn, containing the royal palace, many Thai temples and government offices, has much lower densities than the adjacent Chinese areas for many of the Thais prefer to live in lower density housing in outer suburbs or across the river. On the other hand in a city such as Manila, the Chinese population has tended to move into outer suburbs, leaving the Chinese areas less heavily populated (Figure 17).

In fact the dominantly Filipino areas of Tondo, San Nicolas and Sampaloc have the greatest densities. While direct evidence explaining this pattern is lacking, it may be inferred that this phenomenon has come about because the inner areas, consisting largely of concrete shop-houses, were already over-populated. In addition the Filipino population is poorest in the city. They have been unable to afford rents in the highly-serviced area of the inner core and have therefore moved into the working-class districts of Tondo and Sampaloc where accommodation is cheaper. Their numbers have increased greatly in these areas, bringing about the pattern of population density described above. While it cannot be argued that these examples cited are representative of all the Southeast Asia cities, it is clear that the varying cultural, social and economic patterns of the Southeast Asian countries have prevented close conformity with all elements of the Western pattern.

The two factors which have been the most important determinants of the age and sex characteristics of the Western city have been no less influential in the context of the Southeast Asian city. Thus the character of the urban economy differs radically from the agricultural economy, in that it does not utilize the very young or old and thus concentrates the population in the age group between 15 and 60 years as shown in the accompanying divergency graph of age structures for Kuala Lumpur, Bangkok, Manila and Phnom-Penh (Figure 20). Even more striking is the second factor—the role of internal migration, which shows a heavy concentration in the age groups between 15 years and 40 years. Once again the anomaly imposed by the existence of an alien inner-core population breaks down the pattern of a heavily concentrated labour force in the central core. Thus, as the accompanying maps of the younger age force group (15–24 years) of Bangkok and Manila show, there is a mixed distribution pattern concentrating in different parts of the city. To a large extent such patterns can be explained by the existence of different types of employment and other attracting forces in the city. For example, the concentration of the 15–24 age group in the Ermita Ward of Manila city is largely explained by the existence of schools and universities in this area. Until the plural societies of Southeast Asia begin to break down and new class systems develop, patterns similar to the Western city will not emerge (Figures 18 and 22).

Much of the early urban research on Western cities has pointed to the fact that the process of city growth has been associated with a shift in the numerical balance of sexes from male dominance to female dominance.[4] Research into the demographic character of Latin American cities suggests that this pattern is being repeated in at least one Third World area[5] but as yet (see Table 10) the majority of Southeast Asian cities have sex ratios which are much more heavily weighted in

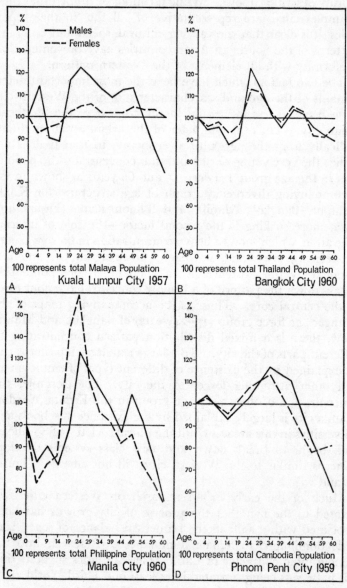

20   Divergency-graph of age structures for selected Southeast Asian cities.

favour of males than their national figures. Only part of this male dominance can be explained by the fact that, with the exception of Cambodia and Indonesia, the national sex ratios have a higher ratio of males to females than is characteristic of most Western countries. Unquestionably more significant is the influence of the immigrant communities who (particularly the Chinese) concentrate in the great cities, for these com-

TABLE 10

SEX RATIOS OF LARGEST CITY AND CAPITAL OR GROUP OF CITIES OF 100,000 +

Country	Year of Census	Males per 100 Females
BURMA	1953	104
Cities of 100,000 +		111
INDONESIA	1961	97
Djakarta		105
SINGAPORE	1947	122
Singapore City		122
THAILAND	1960	104
Cities of 100,000 +		104
FEDERATION OF MALAYA	1957	106
Kuala Lumpur		113
SARAWAK	1947	101
Kuching		106
NORTH BORNEO	1951	107
Sandakan		119
BRUNEI	1951	122
Belait (12,551)		155
PHILIPPINES	1960	101
Manila City		93
CAMBODIA	1959	99
Phnom Penh		105

Sources: Hauser (1957); Biro Pusat Statistik (1963); Thailand Population Census 1960 (1961); Fell (1960); Philippines Census 1960. Summary Report 1963. Tan-kim Huon (1961); Cambodian Census 1959 (1959).

munities often have a highly unbalanced sex ratio heavily weighted in favour of males (see Table 11). Even allowing for these factors, the male dominant sex ratios of the urban areas (with the exception of the Philippines) are largely the result of the dominantly male migration from rural to urban areas.

TABLE II

NUMBERS OF CHINESE IN SELECTED SOUTHEAST ASIAN COUNTRIES
AND SOME FEATURES OF THEIR URBAN CONCENTRATIONS

Country	Date of Population Estimate	Size of Chinese Population	Chinese as a Percentage of Total Population	Percentage of each country's Chinese Population Living in Major Urban Area	Chinese as a Percentage of Total Population Living in Major Urban Area	Sex Ratios of Chinese in Urban Area
Indonesia	1950s	2,500,000	2·5	12·0	10·2	—
Thailand	1960	384,000	1·5	51·3	9·2	155·9
Philippines	1948	250,000	1·0	36·0	3·4	136·3
Burma	1950s	300,000	1·5	24·3	9·5	120·2
Federation of Malaya	1957	2,333,756	37·0	8·3	63·4	103·0
Cambodia	1959	275,000	5·6	22·8	17·6	116·2

Sources: Withington (1963); Thailand Population Census 1960 (1961 and 1962); Philippine Census 1960 (1962 and 1963);
Redick (1961); Fell (1960); Cambodian Census 1959 (1959).

Notes: Accurate contemporary figures of the Chinese in Southeast Asian countries are difficult to locate. Few national
censuses identify the Chinese population by any other form than Place of Birth which means the Chinese populations
are often underestimated in such documents.

This trend is further emphasized by the fact that populations tend to become more masculine as the size of locality increases. This, as the UNESCO Report confirms, '. . . reflects primarily the sex composition of migrants from rural areas and villages to towns and cities'.[6]

A further indication of the male-dominant character of this migration, as well as its age selectivity, can be obtained from the age specific sex ratios shown in Table 12. With the

TABLE 12

RATIO OF MALES TO FEMALES FOR TOTAL POPULATION AND MAIN CITY BY AGE SPECIFIC GROUPS

Philippines (1960)	*Total Population*	*Manila City*
15–24	102·4	73·6
25–34	95·4	92·7
35–44	97·4	96·4
Total Population	101·4	93·2

Cambodia (1959)	*Total Population*	*Phnom-Penh*
15–24	96·3	98·2
25–34	94·3	104·3
35–44	97·5	120·7
Total Population	99·7	105·0

Thailand (1960)	*Total Population*	*Phranakhorn (Bangkok)*
15–24	101·4	108·6
25–34	99·5	106·1
35–44	101·3	108·0
Total Population	100·3	103·7

Federation of Malaya (1957)	*Total Population*	*Kuala Lumpur*
15–24	99·3	117·6
25–34	99·0	116·0
35–44	110·5	123·0
Total Population	106·0	113·0

Sources: Philippine Census 1960 (1962 and 1963); Cambodian Census 1959 (1959); Thailand Population Census 1960 (1961 and 1962); Fell (1960).

exception of the Philippines, all the selected cities show an excess of males in the age groups between 15 and 44. Only in Cambodia (in the age group between 15 and 24 years) is there

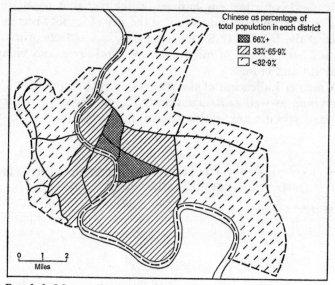

21 Bangkok Metropolitan area. Proportion of Chinese in each census district, 1954.

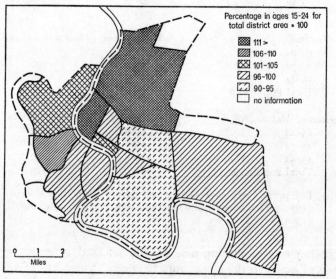

22 Bangkok Metropolitan area. Concentration in ages 15–24, 1960.

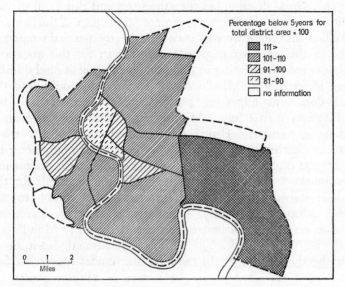

Percentage below 5years for
total district area = 100

111 >
101–110
91–100
81–90
no information

0 1 2
Miles

23 Bangkok Metropolitan area.   Concentration in age group below
5 years, 1960.

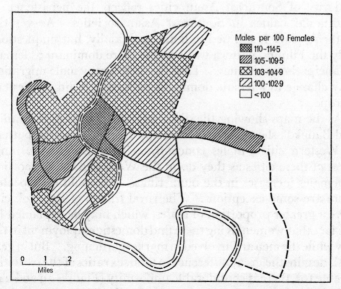

Males per 100 Females

110–114·5
105–109·5
103–104·9
100–102·9
<100

0 1 2
Miles

24 Bangkok Metropolitan area.   Sex ratios by census district, 1960.

roughly equal division between the sexes and this in all proba-
bility represents marriage movement on the part of the females.
The fact that there were over twice as many married women as
men in this age group gives some support for this assertion.
What is most interesting in this table is the exceptional dominance of females in Manila city. There is no doubt that the
male-dominant migration patterns which characterized the
Philippines in 1948 have changed dramatically to a dominantly
female movement. Hunt[7] has outlined some of the main
reasons for this change. First, the growth of manufacturing
in Manila city has created favourable employment opportunities for the females who are frequently more suitable for the
routine assembling and packaging work in the rapidly growing
light industry. Secondly, females who form an increasing
proportion of the college students are attracted to Manila city
with its concentration of higher educational institutions.
Finally, there is no doubt that this movement represents far-
reaching social changes in the nature of Filipino society in
which the equality of sexes is becoming an increasingly important feature. Overall, however, the lack of females in the
majority of Southeast Asian cities reflects the persistence of
traditional values in Southeast Asian societies. As yet the
women's place is still tied to home and family, but unquestionably the Filipino pattern will become more dominant as female
emancipation continues. Thus the dominantly male migration
may change to a female dominant pattern as it did in Western
Europe.

As the maps showing the distribution of sex ratios in Manila
and Bangkok show, there is some approximation to the pattern
of Western cities; males concentrate in general in the inner
cores of these cities as they do in the West, and the proportion
of females increases in the outer rings. As would be expected
there are some exceptions. The rural fringes of Bangkok city
have a greater proportion of males, which may be explained by
the fact that women living there find domestic employment in the
city while the men are involved in market gardening. But in general, despite the great difference in total sex ratios of the two cities
(Table 10), there is considerable uniformity (Figures 19 and 24).

Information on the changes in family life and household

organization is scant and contradictory. Overall it does not suggest that the urban milieu is inducing any radical changes such as occurred in the Western cities. It is important, however, to distinguish between the family and the household. In general a household can be defined as a unit in which an individual or group of individuals share their living quarters and their principal meals. Such households can either be institutional, such as hostels, or private. Families, on the other hand, are groups of persons living together within the same household, who are related by blood or marriage. In general it is the household data which is most amenable to statistical analysis, and which is featured most frequently in statistical sources. There is some evidence that the size of household may be smaller in Southeast Asian urban areas than in the countryside;[8] but this should not be taken as evidence of a desire to limit families. In the Southeast Asian context it represents a reaction against the shortage of housing which prevents large households from forming. In addition the size of household can clearly be affected by the cultural values operating in a society. For instance, the age that children marry and the cultural practices of dwelling with the parents will affect household size. Skinner comments that the Chinese in Bangkok still have an ideal of a large family, while the Thais prefer fewer children.[9] One recurrent feature of the household structure of the Southeast Asian cities is the number which are composed of nuclear families—that is father, mother and children—and other relations who are frequently staying with their kinsfolk in the city while they are being educated or seeking a job. This pattern was particularly prevalent amongst the Malay households the writer studied in Kuala Lumpur.

The contention that the traditional ties of family life are breaking down under the impact of urban life must be looked upon with some doubt if only because of the paucity of concrete studies. Certainly the work of Bruner,[10] Djamour[11] and Skinner does not suggest any radical restructuring of family organization in the urban milieu. There is not even good evidence that the movement of rural families to the city necessarily breaks the kinship ties in the village. Certainly the network of social obligations continues, even though the families may be separated by considerable distances; marriages are arranged, remittances made, and visits are exchanged at the times of celebrations which keep the kinship ties closely knit. Even the single migrants who move to the city tend to rely heavily on kinship ties, associating with, and often living with their kinsfolk.

Van der Kroef[12] has argued in a lengthy essay on the Indonesian town that the circumstances of modern urban society increase social disorganisation and anomie, citing the increasing tension and crime in Djakarta as support for his argument. The facts of his argument cannot be denied; the amazing thing is that, given the problems of the urban environment such as overcrowding, unemployment and housing, even worse social disorganization has not resulted. The persistence of the traditional family unit and of social obligations which act as an important inhibiting control on misbehaviour, is a major factor in keeping the situation from deteriorating. Certainly it cannot be denied that the new work patterns of the city bring about new relationships within the family. The wife of the family is often expected to adopt new roles both in the training of her children and in her relationships with her family. To some extent this new role is brought about by the fact that grandparents, who frequently play an important part in childrearing, are often left behind in the countryside. At the same time city children can often be sent to stay with their grandparents in the countryside to alleviate accommodation or financial pressures in the city. Thus the grandparents' influence in child-rearing is not always destroyed by the movement from countryside to city. The children are, of course, less steeped in traditional values and can adapt to the ways of the city more quickly. It may well be that the pattern of family described in the city is only a transitory phase and will disappear with length of residence in the city. But, as Bruner points out in his study of the Toba Batak in Medan, the traditional family patterns have persisted for sixty years, and there is no evidence of their changing now. The pattern of social relationships in the Southeast Asian city may well represent the evolution of new and distinct forms of urban life, vastly different from the Western patterns.

CONCLUSION

This brief review of the demographic structure of the Southeast Asian city has suggested considerable variation both amongst the cities and from the Western pattern. This is to be expected in such a region of diverse cultural patterns and heterogeneously populated cities, for there is always a close relationship between demographic structure and the culture of a society. It is a little more surprising, however, that given the degree of uniformity in the physical and economic characteristics of the great cities of Southeast Asia, there are not more demographic uniformities. Thus it is clear that while demographic factors such as in-migration to the cities do produce certain uniformities in the demographic structure of the Southeast Asian cities, the mixed ethnic and cultural character of the cities is still the most important reason for the vastly different demographic character of the cities compared to the Western cities.

CHAPTER 7

The Economic Patterns of the Southeast Asian City

INTRODUCTION

THE EXISTENCE of a mono-economic system and an advanced transportation technology in the majority of Western cities have led to a maximum specialization of land use which has most frequently taken the form of concentric circles of relatively homogenous economic usage. The centre of the city is given over to financial and retail uses; outside this core is to be found wholesale and light manufacturing areas interspersed with the homes of working-class groups; surrounding this area is a zone of middle-class homes, and finally there is an outer zone of upper-class residential housing.[1] No such clear zonation characterizes the land use of the large cities of Southeast Asia. The mixed economic structure of the cities in which highly-developed forms of Western capitalism, such as banks and trading firms coexist with pre-industrial and semi-capitalistic forms of economic organizations like the Chinese loan association and the mobile street markets of the indigenous populations, inhibits large areas of homogenous land use from emerging.

Geertz has distinguished between these two economic systems which coexist in the Southeast Asian city in his study of social and economic change in two Indonesian towns.[2] The pre-industrial economy he labels a *bazaar economy*; 'i.e., one in which the total flow of commerce is fragmented into a very great number of unrelated person-to-person transactions'.[3] The central institution of this economy is the market or *pasar*, but as Geertz points out it is only a part of the whole pattern of trading. 'The market place is the climax of this pattern, its focus and centre, but it is not the whole of it; for the *pasar*

style of trading permeates the whole region, thinning out somewhat only in the most rural of villages.'[4]   The second economic
system which can be equated with the term Western capitalism
is a *firm-centred economy* '. . . where trade and industry occur
through a set of impersonally defined social institutions which
organize a variety of specialized occupations with respect to
some particular productive or distributive end'.[5]

Only two zones of land use in the Southeast Asian cities are
relatively constant in their location.   In all the large cities,
the port and its associated complex of wharves and warehouses,
which was the centre of economic activity in the colonial era
retains its supremacy as one of the economic foci of the cities.
Outside the city boundaries a zone of intensive market gardening which supplies much of the fresh meat and vegetables to
the city markets surrounds all the Southeast Asian cities.[6]
Apart from these two zones of relatively homogeneous land use
the remainder of the city is characterized by a tremendous
mixing of economic activity and land use (Figure 25).

Thus the foci of indigenous retailing are the numerous
markets which are scattered throughout the city.   Here in
these great barn-like buildings, crowded with the many peoples
of the city, there are no fixed prices; bargaining and haggling
are part of the ritual of the sale and prices fluctuate dramatically
during the day.   To the Western observer the market is a
place of noise and colour and, as the heat of the tropical day
increases, of overwhelming smell.   The business of the market
begins in the early hours of the morning as trucks and boats
bring vegetables, meat and fish and unload their goods for the
coming day's sales.   By the afternoon the noise and bustle of
the market have quietened, and it is not unusual to see the
stallholders asleep at their empty counters waiting for the next
day.   Surrounding the market are the many street sellers and
shops selling dry goods where the bustle of commercial transactions never seems to stop.   The centres of 'indigenous' retailing
contrast strikingly with the air-conditioned department stores
selling Western-style goods.   Here your feet do not slip on the
melting ice as on the market floor; instead as you walk on the
cool linoleum, the blast of air-conditioning strikes your face.
The goods come from Europe or the United States or Japan;

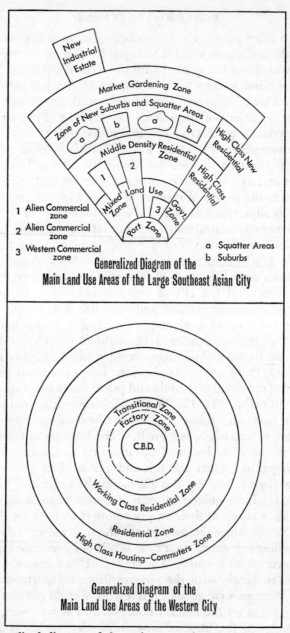

25 Generalized diagram of the main economic zones in the Western city and the Southeast Asian city.

they have fixed prices and a purchase is made without bargaining with a shop assistant who speaks a European language.

Just as these contrasts exist in retailing, so they occur in financing; the branches of Western banks with their fixed rates of interest and loan contrast with the indigenous loan institutions where the whole system of credit raising and loans is different. The contrast exists also in industry with the scattering of small family industry through the city, contrasted with the large-scale Western factory industry confined to specialized estates on the fringes of the city. It is obvious that any attempt to try to discover some general pattern in the distribution of economic activity such as occurs in Western cities is impossible. Perhaps as the transportation systems and the economic structure of the city begin to move towards homogeneity such patterns will occur. But for the present there is little sign of this.

THE PATTERN OF RETAILING & COMMERCE

This juxtaposition of the various types of economic activity reveals itself in the distribution of commercial and retailing activity throughout the city. In crude terms, in most Southeast Asian cities it is possible to distinguish between two main areal concentrations of commerce and retailing. The first of these occurs in all large Southeast Asian cities; it is the Western commercial business district (C.B.D.). As one writer has described this area, it '. . . is the more or less universal metropolis. The wide well-paved streets, large banks, modern hotels and government buildings would be no more or less incongruous in the heart of Sydney or Melbourne.'[7] The architecture of the buildings in Raffles Place in Singapore is English; that in Saigon is French; in Djakarta it is Dutch· Here are found the major hotels serving European food; the movie theatres advertising the latest Western film—where John Wayne and Steve Reeves show the ways of the 'West'. During the daylight hours the European commercial centre is crowded, flowing with office, transport and street workers. Western clothes and Western cars are universal features. French, Dutch or English are common languages spoken in the streets of this area. The banks and the large companies are still mainly foreign-owned and Europeans form an important executive class. Even today, the lower-ranking staff are made up largely of Southeast Asians, the routine of work is based upon European practice, the offices are air-conditioned and the employees work from 9 to 5. The etiquette of the business lunch and chauffeurs calling at 5, to take the tired businessmen to the club, for tennis or golf and the life-saving 'stengah' (whisky and soda), are all part of the European commercial life. The goods sold here are goods made by Europeans for the Westernized taste of the new *élites*—perfumes from France, whisky from Scotland—the best from the West for the wealthiest of the East. A recent addition to the retailing activities of the Western commercial area has been the large garage and car sales shops. Sometimes this activity has been forced to locate itself at some distance from the Western commercial district, because of a shortage of land close to this area. The result is that there is now another focus of Western commercial activity in the Southeast Asian city.

Close by the European commercial zone—sometimes just behind the imposing façade of the air-conditioned office buildings—is the Chinatown or Indian town which may be labelled 'the alien commercial centre'. The pattern of urban commerce is very different in this area. Here small businesses abound: metal makers, jewellers, dressmakers, restaurateurs, chemists, grocers and moneylenders side-by-side. These businesses are located in two-storey shop-houses which frequently serve the triple function of place of residence for the owner, place of manufacture, and place for the sale of goods. In most cases the upper storey of the shop-house is subdivided into tiny rented cubicles. The densities of these 'alien C.B.D.'s are sometimes staggering, frequently reaching figures of over 100,000 per square mile. Here the rhythm of work is very different to that of the European commercial centre. The commerce and industry of the alien commercial centre never seems to stop for people live and work on the same location. They are serviced by street hawkers bringing food and have no need to venture beyond the limits of the alien commercial centre. At night the distinction between the alien commercial centre and the European centre of the cities becomes most striking. The European commercial centre is empty—the dead heart of the city—for, like its Western counterparts, its daytime inhabitants depart to the suburbs where they reside. The alien commercial centre throbs with life long after the European centre stops its activities. Often there are several alien commercial centres scattered throughout the city. Sometimes there are concentrations of retailing and commercial activities for each of the major communities. Thus one finds Indian quarters and Chinatowns, scattered throughout the Southeast Asian cities.

In addition, the occupational concentration of the mixed ethnic populations is also responsible for the diverse pattern of economic activity (see Figure 26[8]). Thus in Phnom-Penh, the commercial core (District 3a) is dominated by the Chinese and other groups who make up the majority of population in the retailing and service sector. To the north (District 2) there is an abrupt change in the character of the city, for this is the main area of government offices in which Cambodians are the chief employees. Across the river (District 7) there are substantial communities of Vietnamese, largely engaged in fishing. In the south, the district in which the royal compound is located, a higher proportion of Cambodians is employed in government services. The fringe districts to the north, west and south of the city are dominated by Cambodians, heavily concentrated in the labourer and artisan employment sector.

Nevertheless, it is false to see these ethnically dominated districts of different economic activity as isolated enclaves which do not interact. The city is an entity—money is its chief means of exchange—all these commercial centres are interrelated.

McIntyre[9] shows the way this interaction operates in Manila city in terms of retailing. He delineates three main types of retailing activity in Manila city:

(i) a proliferation of neighbourhood stores scattered throughout the residential areas. These may be small eating places or small goods stores, but most frequently the typical store is the *sari-sari* store (a Tagalog word roughly equivalent to 'miscellaneous'). He classifies under this neighbourhood shopping pattern the areas of the Malate and Ermita which contain

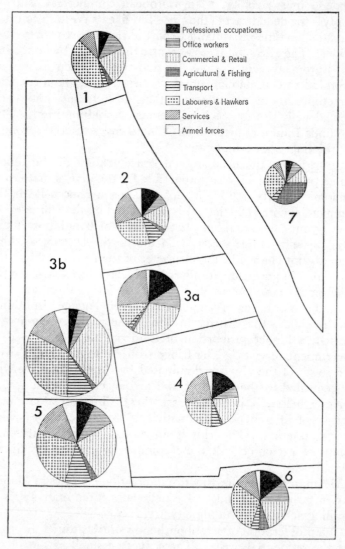

Professional occupations
Office workers
Commercial & Retail
Agricultural & Fishing
Transport
Labourers & Hawkers
Services
Armed forces

26 Phnom-Penh. The distribution of occupations by census district, 1959. District 7 is separated from the remainder of the city by a branch of the Mekong River. The circles are proportionate to the size of work force. The largest circle (District 3b) has 24,540 workers; the smallest circle (District 7) has 5,200 workers.

the Western commercial shops. These are essentially neighbourhood shopping centres for the Europeans and Westernized
élites.[10]

(ii) the groups of retailing stores on the principal thorougr fares
which lead from the city. The chief functional differentiation
distinguishing them from the neighbourhood store type is the
greater variety of products offered. Stores for groceries,
clothing, music, hardware, etc., are characteristic of such
thoroughfare areas.

(iii) the fourteen public markets which McIntyre suggests
form the most important element in the retail pattern of
Manila. The public markets supply most of the perishable
food such as fresh fruits, vegetables, rice, meat and fish. The
ritual of marketing is an important daily occurrence in the life
of the city resident. The rapidly growing population has made
the number of available markets completely inadequate.
Consequently, a sizeable growth of parasite retail concentrations in the surrounding environs has been typical,
and in particular, there has been a rapid postwar rise in
private markets (*talipapas*) to satisfy the need to supply food
for the growing population. The broad types of retailing
which McIntyre describes in Manila can be duplicated in
many other Southeast Asian cities, but a more thorough
analysis will have to await a more detailed investigation of the
diverse patterns of consumption, financing, and economic
organization which make up the retailing and commercial
practices of the Southeast Asian city.

MANUFACTURING IN THE SOUTHEAST ASIAN CITY

This division between 'Western' and 'indigenous' retailing
and commerce also occurs in manufacturing. Most clearly
marked is the division between what may be labelled 'cottage
industries' scattered throughout the city, and the 'Western'
industrial establishments which tend to concentrate in specific
zones, either adjacent to the port (the processing industries of
the colonial era) or in the newly established industrial estates
on the city fringes.

Surveys of the structure and distribution of manufacturing
in the 'great cities' of Southeast Asia are not numerous.

However, Redick's[11] analysis of the 1953 Census of Manufacturing conducted in Rangoon provides some information on the structure and pattern of manufacturing in at least one Southeast Asian city. While it would be hazardous to assume that Rangoon's manufacturing structure is repeated in exact detail in every Southeast Asian city, it does give some indication of the kind of patterns which can be observed in other cities. The results of this survey stress the division between the domestic 'cottage industry' sector and the larger industrial establishments. Thus, of Rangoon's 6,456 industrial establishments engaged in the production of durable and non-durable goods in 1953, 6,045 employed nine or less workers and were classified as 'cottage industries'; 97 per cent of these establishments were family owned and produced goods in the home without the aid of mechanical power; 61 per cent utilized unpaid workers who may be assumed to be largely family workers, and the average number of workers employed was three. These small-scale operatives produced mostly non-durable goods such as food, clothing and cheroots. The remaining industrial establishments were much larger in scale, employing many more workers, using mechanical sources of power, and producing durable goods such as furniture and metal products. The larger of these industries, such as rice and timber processing units, were heavily concentrated along the river front adjacent to the port area. This dual manufacturing structure, representing the juxtaposition of essentially pre-industrial manufacturing production techniques with the Western-orientated industrial establishments, has a clear reflection in the distribution of manufacturing throughout the city. While the proportions of cottage and larger industrial establishments vary from city to city (for instance industrial establishments are much larger and more numerous in Singapore and Malaya), the basic dualism in the manufacturing pattern is repeated in the majority of Southeast Asian cities.

One of the important features of the economic policies of the new governments of Southeast Asia has been their attempt to encourage new industry in an effort to create employment, cut down overseas expenditure on manufactured goods, and correct the warped economic base inherited from the colonial era. While the efforts of these countries to build up industry outside the cities has not always been successful because of problems of political control, the establishment of industry in the large cities has made some progress. This is particularly true of Malaya, Singapore and the Philippines, where the establishment of industrial estates on the fringes of the city is adding a new element to the distribution of economic activity in the city. A good example is the industrial development now being carried on within the satellite town of Petaling Jaya on the fringes of Kuala Lumpur, where by 1963, ten years after its inception, over a hundred factories had been established. The advantages of the concentrated services which such an industrial estate can offer to growing industry—power and water facilities, access by rail and road to near-by Port Swettenham and the existence of a potential labour force in Kuala Lumpur—have certainly proved important inducements to the growth of industry. In addition the Malayan government has offered financial incentives to encourage foreign investment, in the form of tax rebates on pioneer industry. Much of the industry which has been started can be described as light consumer industry, producing such goods as batteries, canned foodstuffs, cement, asbestos products and matches. On the whole the industry does not use labour intensive production techniques, relying rather on a high degree of mechanization and the Western factory organization. It is questionable how adequate this form of industry will be in solving the employment problems of the growing city populations.

It might be useful for some of the Southeast Asian governments to look at the experience of China in this respect, for that country has followed a deliberate policy of turning its back on the former 'colonial cities' such as Shanghai, decentralizing its industry and employing labour intensive techniques wherever possible to make the maximum use of its labour force. Despite the problems of effective utilization of the city labour force, the growth of industrial estates in the cities of Southeast Asia is an important element in bringing the patterns of land use to greater conformity with the model of the Western city.

THE IMPORTANCE OF THE PORT

The one ubiquitous feature of the economic activity of the great cities of Southeast Asia is the significant role that the port and its associated processing industries play. Despite the postwar increase in air traffic, the Southeast Asian countries' contact with the remainder of the world is still largely maritime. The important port functions which the great cities had assumed during the colonial era continue despite independence. As international ports they handle a large proportion of the export and import trade of their territories. Thus Rangoon handles between 80 and 90 per cent of the foreign trade; Bangkok, despite the fact that it has only recently, with the cutting of a new canal, been able to take ocean-going ships of large size, dominates the foreign trade of Thailand; Saigon-Cholon, a tidal river port, was responsible for a sizeable proportion of the rice exports of the Mekong delta until the advent of the recent internal war; and Singapore has always been the principal port for Malaya's exports and imports as well as being the main entrepôt port for the archipelago region. Only Manila has diverged from this pattern of dominance; for example, while some 80 to 85 per cent of the imports pass through the ports of Manila, its proportion of the exports is no more than 30 per cent. The bulkier goods are tending to be shipped from regional ports such as Cebu and Davao. This pattern is repeated on a smaller scale in Indonesia.[12]

While it is clear that there are considerable differences in the type of port, its facilities and the role it plays in the economy of the city, some of the broad features of the ports of Southeast Asia can be well illustrated by Singapore, the largest port and chief entrepôt of Southeast Asia. Singapore has gained this premier status in part because of its position at the cross-roads of Southeast Asia, in part from its status as a free-trade port, but in addition the well established services connected with shipping such as banking, insurance, export and import agencies which have grown up have tended to focus trade on the area. A large proportion of Singapore's national income comes from the services Singapore port performs. The Rueff Report estimated that between 20 and 25 per cent of Singapore's national product is contributed by the entrepôt trade and tourism.[13] The entrepôt trade is said to employ some 70,000, and if the associated port industries are also included, this figure reaches 120–140,000—approximately one-quarter of Singapore's total employment; by far the largest individual employment sector in any of the Southeast Asian port cities.

Singapore, like Manila, has two ports. The older, which consists of the 'roads', the Telok Ayer Basin and the Singapore River, handles most of the primary products such as rice, rubber, copra and coffee which have come from neighbouring countries. In addition, the consumer goods which have come from Western countries, as well as Hong Kong, China, and Japan are unloaded here to be transhipped to other Southeast Asian countries. The new port consists of the Singapore Harbour Board wharves. Here are berthed the passenger ships and large ocean-going boats which load the primary products processed in Singapore. There is also an important concentration of indigenous shipping traffic, consisting largely of trading schooners from the Celebes and other Indonesian Islands in the Rochore River area.[14] This indigenous trade is essentially a carry-over of the trade that dominated the region in the fifteenth and sixteenth centuries.

Surprisingly, the storage and loading operations carried out in the Port of Singapore are extremely complex. The entrepôt goods are not stored in one area as in many trading centres, but are scattered throughout the commercial quarter in godowns (warehouses) and shops. While there are storage facilities at the wharves of the Singapore Harbour port, they are not large enough to hold the volume of the entrepôt trade. With such a great variety of traders, semi-wholesalers and agency houses involved in the process of loading, unloading and storage, it is not surprising that there is an extreme diversity of labour employment practices.[15] The stevedores work the flat barges which unload the boats in the roads; the dock labour is employed by the Singapore Harbour Board; the godown labour is responsible for unloading the barges and storing the goods, and a vast number of people are involved in shifting the goods throughout the city. The work of the port is the life-blood of Singapore.

Recently the Port of Singapore has been facing a series of crises which threaten to reduce its importance. Internally, the attempts to rationalize the techniques of unloading, storage, and labour employment have not been notably successful. An even greater problem was posed for a period by the Confrontation policy of Indonesia which led to a substantial reduction in the port's income from the Indonesian entrepôt trade. With the end of Confrontation it may be assumed that trade with Indonesia will recommence, but it will take a considerable time for it to assume the importance of the pre-Confrontation period. Singapore's role as the chief entrepôt port of the colonial era probably could not have persisted in this postwar era, and it is not surprising therefore that the present government is pushing ahead as rapidly as possible with industrialization policies.

CONCLUSION

While it is clear that developments in the postwar era are bringing about some changes in the distribution of economic activity in the large Southeast Asian city, the *transitional* nature of the economic structure of the cities in which *bazaar-type* economy coexists with a *firm-type* economy, prevents all but a few zones of homogenous economic usage emerging. It is significant that the most clearly demarcated zones of economic activity which have emerged in the postwar period—the new industrial estates and the car selling areas—are both largely integrated within the *firm-type* economy. In addition, the rapid growth of population, the creation of large squatter settlements and the slow development of transportation have also hindered the concentration of economic activity. Perhaps the movement away from the bazaar-type economy to the firm-type economy which Geertz had observed in Modjokuto will eventually bring about a pattern of land use which resembles the Western city, but for the present the mixed and seemingly chaotic distribution of land use prevails.

CHAPTER 8

The Residential Patterns of the Southeast Asian City

IT IS as hard to generalize about the patterns of residence in the Southeast Asian city as it is to generalize about the location of economic activity. Nevertheless, the persistence of residential patterns established during the colonial era, together with the rapid growth of cities in the last fifteen years, has imposed certain common patterns of residence in virtually all the larger cities. The major element of the colonial city was the mosaic of ethnic quarters—the tightly packed shop-house areas of the Chinese, the spacious low-density 'compounds' of the Europeans, and the rural-like villages of the indigenous population scattered around the fringes of the city. The rapid growth of the population of the cities in the postwar era, associated with the socio-economic changes which are creating an emergent middle class, have caused a proliferation of squatter settlements in the interstices and fringes of the city, as well as the growth of Western-type suburbs, adding new elements to the residential ecology of the city. In the process some of the lines between the various racial enclaves of the city have become a little blurred, but overall ethnic concentration is still responsible for the major divisions in the residential areas of the city.

At first sight it might appear that the dominating role of cultural and ethnic pluralism, together with the embryonic development of a class structure similar to that of the Western city makes comparison with a Western city model invalid. But it must not be forgotten that many Western cities have possessed populations which were racially and culturally as mixed as the populations of the present-day Southeast Asian city. Indeed, it is only necessary to read a selection of the many community studies of Chicago in the nineteen-twenties and thirties to realize this fact.[1] What is different in the Southeast Asian city is the fact that the class structure at present shows little conformity with the Western city. The research of Burgess on the North American city postulated a direct relationship between social class and distance from the centre of the city, with the working class living closest to the city core and the upper class in the city fringes. Such a model would seem to have only marginal validity in the context of Southeast Asian urbanism.[2] Historically, as Sjoberg[3] has shown, the *élite* have always lived close to the city core, while the poorer population fans out towards the periphery; it is only with the development of fast transport and a more stratified class structure that the North American patterns of class residence emerge. It might be suggested that the patterns of residence of the Southeast Asian city which include a mixture of the poorest and wealthiest elements of the city in both the core and outer areas, represent some transitory phase which is developing between the patterns of pre-industrialism and industrialism.

Some elements in the history of the large Southeast Asian cities support such an assertion, for the patterns of residence established in the colonial city were basically pre-industrial, in that the city *élite* (in this case the European administrators and businessmen) lived close to the centre in carefully demarcated areas. However, the rapid influx of alien immigrants and their concentration close to the city soon drove the Europeans away from the rowdy city core to spacious compounds some distance away. This certainly was the case in Batavia, Singapore and Rangoon, although not to such an extent in Manila and Kuala Lumpur where the river formed a barrier against the encroachment of the alien population. It can be argued that such a process of residential deconcentration represents a desire of the European *élites* to be separated socially and geographically from the mass of the city population, rather than the consequences of improvements in transportation technology such as occurred in the Western city. Thus the process of suburbanization was occurring in the colonial city even before the Western city, but for very different reasons. Furthermore, the persistence of the pre-industrial practice of combining work and residence, associated with the segregative patterns induced by the strength of community ties, prevented the suburbanization of the remainder of the city population. The end-product of the colonial period was to freeze the various communities in distinct quarters; and it is this basic pattern which persists until this day.

The considerable growth of population in the postwar era, has however, induced some changes in the residential patterns established during the colonial period. The influx of population filled the inner areas of the city to saturation point and then spilled over into a series of squatter colonies on the city fringes. The change in political power has seen the former areas of government housing which the Europeans had occupied taken over by the indigenous bureaucrats. In addition, new government housing areas have been created for the proliferating civil service of these new countries, who are also increasingly occupying the new middle-class suburbs. Thus the rapid urban growth of the Southeast Asian cities has merely added new elements to the city rather than transforming the colonial residential pattern.

RESIDENTIAL PATTERNS—Manila City

The manner in which these residential patterns emerge in the Southeast Asian city can be well illustrated by reference to Manila city in the Philippines and Kuala Lumpur, the booming capital of the Federation of Malaysia. In the case of Manila city, one of the oldest 'Western' cities in Southeast Asia, the extensive damage suffered at the end of the war could have provided the opportunity for extensive replanning which would have radically redesigned the old colonial city. Instead, the patterns of residence were only slightly modified by the influx of the population. Basically, there are four main residential quarters each distinguished by the mode of housing, class and ethnic group of the population residing there. As Figures 27, 28, 29, 30 and 31 show most clearly distinguishable, by the type and quality of housing, are the districts of Santa Cruz, Binondo, San Nicolas, Quiapo and San Miguel. The core of

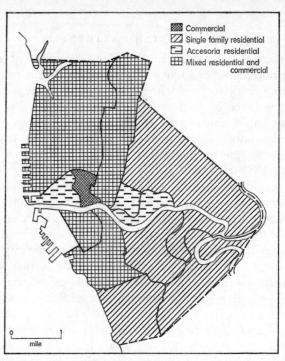

Commercial
Single family residential
Accesoria residential
Mixed residential and commercial

27 Manila city. Major types of building. An accesoria is a one- or two-floor structure divided into many dwelling units.

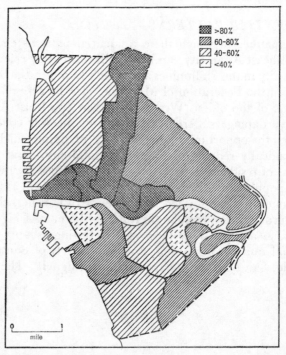

>80%
60–80%
40–60%
<40%

28. Manila city. Percentage of buildings constructed of strong materials.

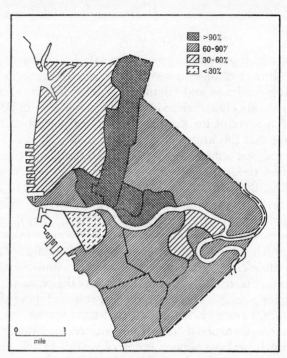

29　Manila city.　Percentage of occupied dwellings with flush toilet.

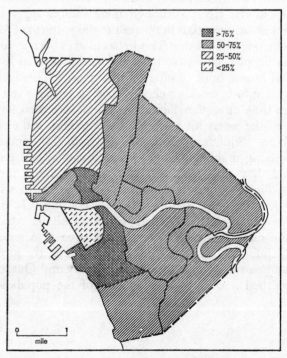

30　Manila city.　Percentage of occupied dwellings with a radio.

this area, which possesses a mixed population, is the dominantly Chinese district of Binondo with its characteristic shop-houses combining residence and commerce. The districts surrounding Binondo are characterized by the 'accessoria' or buildings of flats which account for the high density of population. It is significant that this area, along with some districts south of the river, is the best serviced with piped water and toilet facilities. The second residential area, which is distinguished largely by its dominantly Filipino population, encompasses the rest of the city with the exception of the Ermita district. While the indices portrayed on the maps are not perfect,[4] they do suggest that there is an important contrast between working-class districts such as Tondo, Intramuros and Pandacan and the lower middle-class areas such as Sampaloc and Santa Ana. In the former districts the low percentage of the population who have higher education indicates the low status of these districts. In addition, housing is much poorer, with a low percentage of the houses constructed of strong materials. While radio ownership is perhaps a poor index of wealth in the Japanese transistor-saturated markets of Southeast Asia, it is significant that Tondo and Intramuros share the lowest rates of radio ownership in the city. Although these indices suggest some emergent class differentials in the residential patterns of Manila, it should be pointed out that Tondo has always been a working-class area peopled by native labourers and fishermen living in traditional houses built of nipa and bamboo. The decline of Intramuros into a working-class district was more the result of chance than any other factor, for the old Spanish fort area was one of the worst hit areas in the bombing of the Second World War. Squatters quickly moved into the bombed out ruins, building makeshift homes of tin, bamboo and packing-cases, and they still remained there at the time of the 1960 census.[5] Finally, there is the district of Ermita, in which is located the university and better class housing. It has the highest percentage of population who have higher education, and is the most Westernized residential area of Manila city. While the information is not shown on the maps, the surrounding urban areas of Manila city such as Pasay and Quezon city have absorbed a considerable amount of the population increase. Suburban projects for the emergent middle class have proliferated in these outlying districts, along with huge squatter encampments. While the limitations of data prevent definitive conclusions being drawn, it is clear that in Manila prewar

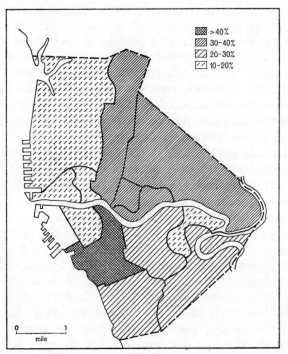

31 Manila city. Percentage of population in each district with higher education. Higher education is defined as the completion of high school or college education.

patterns have persisted, being only slightly modified by the growing population and emergent social structure of the city.

CHANGING RESIDENTIAL PATTERNS—A Case Study of Kuala Lumpur[6]

The study of the changing residential patterns in Kuala Lumpur, the capital of the Federation of Malaysia and the growing middle-class dormitory suburb of Petaling Jaya offer

K   145

a useful comparison with Manila city, if only because Malaya received its independence later than the Philippines and this gives us the opportunity to study the changes in the residential patterns of a society prior to independence. In 1947 Kuala Lumpur exhibited the characteristic residential patterns of a colonial town. The long-established enclaves of the various ethnic groups were concentrated on the flat alluvial valley of the Klang River, forming a mosaic of social and cultural worlds. The tightly packed shop-house area of Chinatown; the principal area of Malay settlement—Kampong Bharu; and the areas of Indian settlement, such as Sentul and Brickfields, were the cultural and residential and occupational foci of a great mass of the city's population. On the hilly areas to the west of the city, the main compounds of the European administrators were located. Finally the period of the Japanese invasion had reduced the control of the municipal authorities to such an extent that many squatters were able to move into the city and settle in ethnically segregated kampongs, in vacant land within the city and on its periphery.

The rapid increase in the population of the city in the period between 1947 and 1957 theoretically should have produced a situation in which the ethnic enclaves were broken down and greater mixing occurred. But as Figure 32 shows the ethnic centres still persisted in 1957. New residential elements, however, had been added. First and foremost, the rate of building did not keep pace with the growth of population, and consequently the squatter settlements from 1947 on greatly increased in number. One estimate in 1954 placed the squatter population of Kuala Lumpur as high as 140,000, almost half of the city's population, and while this figure may be slightly exaggerated, this proliferation of illegal housing gave the city a truly rural appearance for it broke down the physical barriers between the clearly demarcated zones of ethnic residence. By 1957 *élite* area and squatter area often existed side by side. Secondly, there was a considerable growth of Western-type suburbs, particularly on the hilly areas to the west which now became the chief area of the new mixed middle class of government civil servants (mainly Malay), wealthy Chinese businessmen and the European

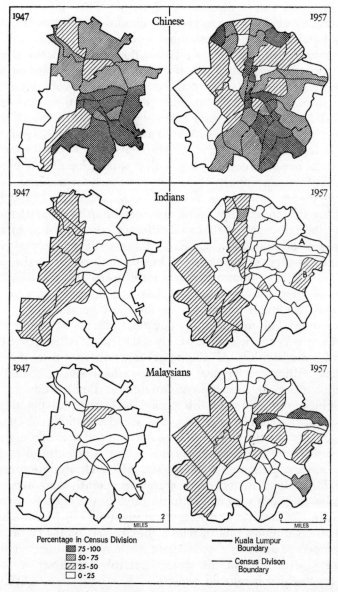

32 Distribution of ethnic groups in Kuala Lumpur city, 1947 and 1957.

managerial and diplomatic groups. The mixed ethnic character of the area emerges prominently in Figure 32. The final residential elements added to the city resulted from the extension of the city's boundaries, the unstable political conditions existing during this period of colonial devolution, and the desire to solve some of the city's housing problems. The extension of the city's boundaries incorporated several small rural Malay villages, and more significantly several Chinese 'new villages', such as Ayer Panas, made up of resettled squatters from outside the city boundaries. One of the largest of these new villages, Jinjang, with a population of over 20,000 has become an important dormitory suburb for the city. The burgeoning squatter populations also forced the municipal authorities to attempt some schemes of urban resettlement, but the cultural resistance of different ethnic groups to new types of housing did not permit the resettlement areas to be mixed in their populations. Thus there were two main types of resettlement housing built—multi-storey flat dwellings for the Chinese and Indians, and detached housing units for the Malays on small lots which would allow vegetable and fruit growing. The major multi-storey flat scheme was built close to the city centre while the Malay resettlement scheme occurred (in Census division (A), Figure 32) some distance from the city. These cultural preferences in housing effectively segregated the ethnic groups in the supposed 'mixing bowl' of the city.

The end product of this period of substantial population growth, boundary expansion, and social and political change was to disturb the basic ethnic patterns of the city only slightly. The desire to live amongst people of the same cultural preferences, race, language and religion, effectively inhibited racial mixing. Such factors were certainly operative amongst the Malay migrants who moved to the city, for the majority moved first to the familiar and long-established area of Malay settlement—Kampong Bharu, where they rented rooms before the cramped conditions forced them to move to other areas of Malay settlement in the city. Certainly proximity to work was a decisive factor, for while the transport systems of Kuala Lumpur were by no means inadequate, the additional expense incurred in travelling was an important factor causing squatter settlements to grow up close to places of employment. But even these settlements were divided into a mosaic of different ethnic quarters. The emergence of an ethnically mixed bureaucratic class did bring about some racial mixing in such government housing areas as Kampong Pandan (Census division (B)), where the lower grade government servants were forced to mix residentially because of the provision of government housing. Some mixing also occurred in the *élite* suburbs of the western hills. The difference in grades of housing as related to the concentration of ethnic groups and topography is shown clearly in Figure 33 which is a cross-section of Kuala Lumpur. In the new *élite* area of Kenny Hill, rents average $500 Malayan monthly, and the 'other races' groups (of which the European make up nearly two-thirds) constitute over 30 per cent of the total population. The rental per month drops rapidly on the lowland flood plains of the Batu and Gombak Rivers, and in the traditional areas of ethnic concentration of Chinese and Malaysians—Tiong Nam Settlement and Kampong Bharu, average rents are in the vicinity of $150 per month. Rentals and the standard of housing increase again in the Ampang Road–Court Hill–Golf View Road area to $500 Malayan per month.

To conclude this brief analysis it is clear that the basic patterns of ethnic segregation are only slowly breaking down in the Manila and Kuala Lumpur areas. While the growing middle class has tended to be responsible for the growth of Western-type suburbs, the swamping of the cities by rural migrants has reinforced rather than weakened the residential patterns of the colonial era.

The spatial mixing of the various residential types in the Southeast Asian cities makes the task of mapping distinct residential areas exceptionally difficult. Nevertheless, it is possible to suggest three main residential zones each of which poses distinct problems of planning within the wider context of overall city planning. The characteristics and problems of the first two of these zones—the overcrowded slum quarters of the long established population and the illegal makeshift housing of the rapidly growing squatter populations will be dealt with in Chapter 9. In this chapter the characteristics

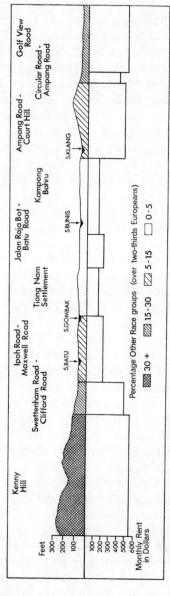

33 Vertical profile across Kuala Lumpur city, relating relief, monthly rent and concentration of other race groups, 1957.

of the third type—the Western-type suburbs of the emerging middle class will be described by reference to one area—the dormitory suburb of Petaling Jaya, some five miles from Kuala Lumpur (see Figure 34).

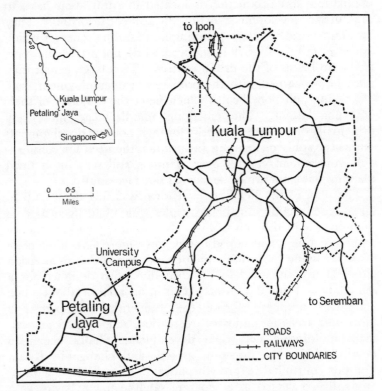

34 The location of Petaling Jaya in relation to Kuala Lumpur city, Federation of Malaysia.

PETALING JAYA—A Middle Class Suburb of Malaysia[7]

The study of Petaling Jaya also provides the opportunity to evaluate a concrete example of town planning in a Southeast Asian city. The solutions presented by town planners to combat the problems of housing and urban amenities for a rapidly increasing population are numerous. They range from negative measures such as laws which would prevent people from moving into the city, to revolutionary plans for the radical decentralization of urban centres by the establishment of a network of new towns.[8]   In fact most national governments faced with the reality that the majority of their population and production is located in rural areas have to rank urban development low on the scale of priorities.   They are thus forced to adopt planning and housing schemes which are essentially palliative in nature and do not attack the roots of the problems of the urban centres.   To a large extent they must be concerned with the problems of unemployment, lack of housing and poor health which beset the majority of their city populations.   The emerging middle class must rely principally on private enterprise for their housing development; but as the study of Petaling Jaya shows, the need for considerable government control over planning still remains if town planning schemes are to be carried out successfully.

The plan of the Petaling Jaya town was first drawn up in 1950, based mainly on the principles which had been used in planning the British new towns.   By combining work, residence and recreation it was hoped to develop a more agreeable mode of urban living than that which characterized the great Asian city.   It was intended to be a satellite town designed for a self-contained population of 70,000 in an area of about 3,000 acres with numbers of connected residential neighbourhood units and areas for industry, recreation, schools and government buildings.   Yet when development finally began in Petaling Jaya, the forces of growth and change in Kuala Lumpur controlled its growth patterns.   Thus Petaling Jaya, originally conceived as a separate satellite town, began as a squatter resettlement scheme, and it was only later with the availability of loan finance for private home construction and the surge of a demand for better quality suburban housing that Petaling Jaya came to resemble the middle-class Westernized suburb.   The industrial area of the town was slow to attract factories, and it was not until after independence that they began to grow.

The rather haphazard and ill-planned settling of the town effectively prevented the original aims from being achieved. Thus the first settlers, poor Chinese squatters, were shifted from Kuala Lumpur in 1951 to make way for a housing development scheme, and moved to hastily constructed homes of poor quality in the south of the present town. While the roading and urban amenities such as piped water and sewage were adequate, the original aims of high density housing were put aside in the haste of building semi-detached housing units. The major unskilled labour was to come from here for the projected industry in the town, but the numbers were never large enough. By 1954 the administrative reorganization of the town led to the freeing of land for middle-class housing requirements and from that date on, with the exception of some terraced housing, detached bungalows set in the middle of an eighth of an acre have been predominant.

As a planned town Petaling Jaya has many features which set it apart from the other Malayan centres. The Western observer at once notices its physical similarity to a Western suburb. The absence of any large shop-house area and the uncharacteristic separation of the residential, commercial and industrial functions are also distinguishing features. There are two commercial town centres. The first is known as Petaling Lama, or old Petaling and is located close to sections 1 and 2, the earliest settled areas. This was the first commercial area developed and only recently has the new centre, which is intended to act as the main commercial centre of the town been built. Despite the recency of the second commercial centre, it is already becoming a recognizable shopping centre for the middle-class population of the town, with air-conditioned restaurants and grocery shops offering a wide range of Western goods, while Petaling Lama offers many of the types of goods which can be purchased in the Chinatown of any Asian city. The other clearly demarcated zone is that devoted to industry which has grown rapidly since 1957, located to the north and west of the town where there is easy access to the main roads leading to Kuala Lumpur and Port Swettenham.

The physical similarity of Petaling Jaya to the suburbs of the Western cities has led some to observe that the way of life of its inhabitants is Westernized as well. An analysis of the socio-economic structure of the town, indicates certain similarities between the Petaling Jaya dweller and the Western suburban-ite, particularly in terms of their possession of the material signs of suburban affluence—refrigerators, cars, etc.—but over-all there are marked differences. The majority of the town's inhabitants are middle-class bungalow dwellers, largely engaged in white collar occupations such as banking, business, govern-ment service and schoolteaching. Their incomes are much higher than the Malayan average, in cases exceeding $550 Malayan per month. The other part of the town's population is made up largely of unskilled workers and their families living in more densely populated areas, where they have been shifted by the government.

Ethnically the town, like the majority of Malaya's urban areas, is populated largely by Chinese who make up two-thirds of the population. With the exception of a small group of Europeans, the rest of the town's population is equally divided between the Malays and Indians. The multi-racial structure of the dormitory suburb effectively prevents a homogenous pattern of life, similar to that of Western suburbs from emerg-ing, although there is some evidence that there is some inter-ethnic mixing on the social level in clubs and other such institutions. There is, however, very little inter-ethnic visiting even amongst people who live next door to each other which suggests that ethnic differences may inhibit the growth of a neighbourliness similar to that of Western suburbs. Much of the communication between the various groups is carried on in English, despite the attempts of the Malaysian government to introduce Malay as the main language medium. But within the home the ethnic groups' vernacular language is generally used. The picture of life which emerges in this suburb indicates that the move towards Western urban patterns of life is only just beginning.

Many other middle-class suburbs similar to Petaling Jaya have grown up in the cities of Southeast Asia, but it is difficult to know if similar patterns are emerging. Suffice to say that the newest element of the social ecology of the Southeast Asian city is still in a phase of transition in which traditional and Western patterns of life coexist.

CHAPTER 9

Slums and Squatters in the Southeast Asian City

INTRODUCTION

THE URBAN population explosion of the postwar period has caused burgeoning problems of unemployment, inadequate housing and transportation which have brought some of the cities to the verge of urban anarchy. To the Western visitor the evidence of these problems is only too obvious. The breakdown of public transportation is evidenced by the frustrating lack of any time-table. The overcrowded buses pick their way through streets cluttered with pedestrians, bicycles, motor scooters and motor cars. The problems of unemployment and under-employment are obvious in the presence of beggars, touts, and superfluous shop attendants who hover in the vicinity of any potential purchaser. Most obvious, however, is the lack of adequate housing for the city dwellers. Strikingly so because the shack settlements and teeming tenements appear in such contrast to the cities of the West. Obvious, too, because of the glaring contrasts in the styles and quality of housing. The juxtaposition of the affluent *élites* in the spacious Western housing in the cooler hilly suburbs, with new roads and the status symbols of affluence such as the American car, contrast with the neglect and shabbiness of the flimsy, miserable huts of the squatter colonies and the overcrowded noisy tenements.

If the Western observer should wish to put these problem areas out of his mind as evidence of a purely temporary inability to provide enough housing in the face of rapid population increase—a purely temporary phenomenon which 'crash housing schemes' will solve—he should take care, for the 'slums' of the industrial city of western Europe and North

America still exist. In fact the squatter settlements and slums of the Southeast Asian city are symptoms of much wider problems in the societies of Southeast Asia; problems for which the piecemeal provision of housing can be little more than a palliative measure; problems which are the result of the failure of the majority of the Southeast Asian nations to develop overall policies of economic development to facilitate a balance in the flow of investment and people between the rural and urban sectors.[1]

The unique facet of the housing problem posed by the rapid growth of Third World cities, as compared to the Western experience, is the dominant role played by squatter settlement. As Abrams[2] has pointed out, in the West the squatter process was associated with the growth of rural settlement; the slum with the formation of the industrial city. In Southeast Asia it is the squatter settlements which are the symptom of modern city growth. At the same time, the Southeast Asian city has not avoided the evil of the slum tenement; the overcrowded Chinatown is an ubiquitous feature of Southeast Asia. Thus the process of city growth in Southeast Asia is saddled with the double evil of slum and squatter settlement. The combined population of these areas frequently makes up two-thirds of the total population of the cities of Southeast Asia, so the problems affect the whole city.

Some care has been taken so far to distinguish between slum and squatter settlement as distinct types of substandard housing problem areas in the city. While it is perfectly correct to label squatter settlements 'slums', for they do represent areas of physically decrepit housing which lack basic amenities such as electric light, water, sanitation and adequate roads, it can be suggested that they are quite distinct from slum areas which have an overcrowded population and legal status of ownership. More important is the danger that if a common definition is accepted for both types of area, then a common solution can be offered. It is the writer's contention that the slum and the squatter settlements are distinct from each other and that different solutions must be put into practice for their problems. The remainder of this chapter elaborates this argument, illustrated by case studies.

SQUATTER SETTLEMENT—in the Cities of Southeast Asia

Abrams in his pioneer study of the housing problems of the Third World city distinguishes between two principal types of squatter.[3] The first type, the 'street sleeper', the 'mobile squatter without a house', is not common in the cities of Southeast Asia, although isolated examples occur in all the major cities. The overall numbers of squatters is in no way comparable to that of the cities of India where, in Calcutta for instance, it is estimated that some 600,000 people sleep on the streets. The second type of squatter—the man who illegally occupies land and builds his home on it—is far more common in Southeast Asia. While lack of comprehensive data prevents any total estimate of the total number of squatters, scattered figures from some Southeast Asian cities give an idea of the size of this significant element. Thus in 1961 there was an estimated 750,000 squatters in Djakarta (25 per cent), 100,000 in Kuala Lumpur (25 per cent); in 1963 some 320,000 in Manila city (23 per cent) and in Singapore from 200,000 to 250,000 (approximately 26 per cent). When it is realized that these estimates only record the squatter populations within city boundaries and that there is a sizeable squatter population living outside the city, it can be seen that the total population of squatters in the Southeast Asian cities is very large indeed.[4]

Other factors beside the rapid growth of city populations have also contributed to the growth of these squatter settlements. The disorder which occurred after the Japanese defeat, while the new civil administrations were struggling to establish themselves, provided the opportunity for many squatters to occupy land, particularly bomb-damaged areas, which they might not have been able to do if the civil administrations had been functioning effectively. This occurred, for instance, in the inner core area of Manila city within the walls of the old Spanish fort of Intramuros. In addition, the shortage of food in the city during the Japanese occupation had forced many city dwellers to move out beyond city limits to practice subsistence farming. Some of these people did not choose to move back into the city again. The period of

Japanese occupation which allowed the squatter to grab a foothold in his illegal occupation of land in the city was followed by a similar period of disorganization in the early years of independence, when political instability in the country side, together with enfeebled control in the large cities, allowed the city populations to occupy illegally land at their will. The lack of finance for urban development programmes, associated with the potential political power of the squatters, prevented city governments from removing them and these settlements have grown increasingly to be a major element in the present day city.

There appears to be no common location for these settlements. Dwyer has suggested in a study of some squatter settlements in Asia, that these areas differ considerably from those in Latin American cities because '... their growth on the peripheries of the cities has been limited by the fact that the land is often intensely cultivated up to the city limits and squatters have therefore penetrated in large numbers to the hearts of the cities. ...'[5] It seems a doubtful assertion because while squatter settlements may be found in many of the core of Southeast Asian cities they also occupy the fringes of such cities as Manila, Djakarta, Kuala Lumpur and Rangoon. The appearance of the squatter settlements varies a great deal. As the accompanying photographs show, some, such as the Malay squatter settlements in Kuala Lumpur, retain a rural appearance with the houses exact replicas of those found in the rural areas. In squatter areas such as these, while there is an absence of urban amenities, there is no real overcrowding; in fact there is enough space for the squatters to possess quite sizeable gardens. Other areas, such as the squatter settlements which existed in the Intramuros area, are much more crowded and the housing is of very poor quality; they are replicas of the Bidonvilles of Algeria or the 'favelas' of Rio de Janeiro. There are even some floating squatter colonies where populations live in junks and boats.[6] In general it may be said that wherever some degree of political and legal security is offered to the squatter, the standard of housing improves. For example, in the city of Davao in the Philippines the Mayor gave in to the demands of the squatters and legalized occupation of the land. The result has improved the social status of the owners and quality of housing of the former squatter areas.[7] Despite the considerable differences in the physical appearance of the squatter areas throughout Southeast Asia, they share certain common features. They all lack the public amenities common to the urban environment. Sanitation and water supplies are virtually non-existent so many squatter settlements are located close to rivers and run the risk of frequent flooding but have a ready-made water and sewerage system. Occasionally, however, the municipal authorities, horrified at the health consequences of this practice, run standing pipelines into the squatter area.

The lack of physical amenities and the poor standard of housing which characterize the squatter areas presents many safety and health hazards. While the inadequate diets and the lack of medical care forced on the squatters by their poverty contribute to the high occurrence of disease and death, the milieu of the area characterized by unsanitary, overcrowded housing is also an aggravating factor. A less frequent but no less dangerous hazard is fire. The lack of piped water, the incendiary nature of the attap roofs of the squatter settlements, and the prevalence of wood cooking fires combine to ensure that fires, once started, completely destroy these settlements. It has been estimated that more than 70 per cent of the fires in Manila city occur in the squatter areas, and such figures can be duplicated in many other Southeast Asian cities. A final hazard is the widespread crime in these areas. Van der Kroef describes the groups of Djakarta 'djembel-djembel' (vagabonds) who are responsible for much of the crime in the city as living in the squatter settlements or vagabond villages.[8] Amongst the squatters such criminals find ready targets for petty extortion of recruits for their gangs. Fear of eviction; fear of fire; fear of crime—fear is the governing force of the squatter area.

It is difficult to generalize about the socio-economic status of squatter dwellers. Suffice to say that in general they represent the most recent and the poorest of the city's population. The inhabitants are the mendicants of the city—the betcha drivers, the dock workers, the building labourers and of course, the unemployed. It is to these areas that the new migrants to the city move. The Indonesian novelist, Mochtar Lubis, describes how Saimun, a poor labourer moved to a squatter area:

> He remembered how in the first weeks after his arrival in Djakarta he wept when the evening came and he knew not where to wander any more, and looked for a place to sleep under the awning of a shop. Until he met Itam who befriended him and they got work as garbage-removing coolies. And later they were able to rent lodgings in the hut of Pak Idjo, the driver of a delaman pony-cart. Just one room, next to the room where Pak Idjo slept with his old wife and their three children. But the hunger which gnawed at his guts never ceased, and the weariness in his bones never really went away.[9]

It is true that in some squatter colonies people who have managed to upgrade their socio-economic status and income choose to remain in the areas, often becoming owners and landlords of rented housing.

Finally, these squatter populations pose an important political problem for the municipal and national governments of the Southeast Asian nations. Attempts to evict the squatter populations, even when alternative housing is provided, arouse tremendous resentment and have precipitated large-scale riots. In the end it may well be that many of the Southeast Asian governments will be forced to accept the fact that the best solution is to give the squatters legal ownership of their land.

The following case study of a kampong which the author studied in 1962–63 illustrates the characteristics of one squatter area in some detail.

KAMPONG SETOR—a Case Study of a Squatter Settlement

The broad features of Kuala Lumpur's rapid growth in population in the period between 1947 and 1957 have been described in Chapter 8. All the ethnic communities making up the multi-racial society of Kuala Lumpur contributed to this growth which was roughly proportionate to their various populations in the city, with the exceptions of the Malays who more than doubled. The ethnic groups who moved to the city shared common problems of employment, assimilation to the life of the city and inadequate housing, but the problem of housing was particularly difficult for the Malays because their community formed such a small part of the total city population and therefore their rapid influx soon exhausted any available housing in the Malay quarters of the city. Thus many of the Malay migrants to the city were forced to move into squatter settlements, and by 1961 almost half the Malay community were living in ethnically concentrated squatter settlements scattered throughout the city.[10] One such settlement was Kampong Setor, located close to the core of the city, squeezed between the Gombak River and the railway line which ran north from the city. Situated close by and up a steep embankment was the Prime Minister's residence. As the crow flies, the distance between the Prime Minister's home and Kampong Setor was little more than one hundred yards, but the distance in terms of Malayan society represented a climb from the lowest rank of Malayan society to the top-most rung of the social ladder (Figure 35).

The exact size and extent of Kampong Setor was difficult to establish. Most of the Malay squatter areas merged indistinguishably into each other, and the kampong boundaries were generally delineated by which surau (praying mosque) the inhabitants attended. Kampong Setor had no surau; its inhabitants generally went to Kampong Bharu, a near-by large, legal Malay settlement, for religious meetings; and thus it was almost impossible to establish its territorial limits, especially to the north where it merged into another Malay squatter settlement, Kampong Maxwell. A preliminary count estimated some seventy houses.

In 1962 in the course of a much larger survey of the Malay community in Kuala Lumpur, 23 of these households were interviewed in an attempt to collect information on the broad socio-economic characteristics of the squatter community. The 23 households which were interviewed lived in 21 separate dwelling units. Two of the dwelling units were subdivided in such a manner as to allow an additional household to dwell in the unit. The houses were all built in Malay style, elevated on stilts with wood walls and in most cases tin roofs. Eleven of the houses were owned by the occupiers, and the other 12 rented. In these houses lived a population of 103 people consisting of 54 males and 49 females. The simple family was the basic household unit; 20 out of the 23 consisted of married couples plus children; one household was made up of

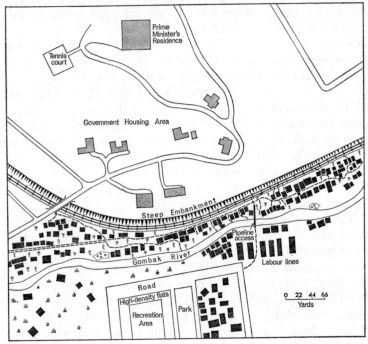

35 Plan of Kampong Setor. A Malay squatter area in Kuala Lumpur city.

a married couple without children; and two households consisted of single men. Many of the simple families were recently married and had very young children. This is revealed in the age structure of the kampong which has over one-third of its population below 5 years and another 25 per cent concentrated in the age group between 21 and 35. The age structures were thus heavily weighted in the migratory and young age brackets.

An analysis of the migratory histories and past residence of the household heads of Kampong Setor cast some doubts on the stereotyped picture of the rural migrant moving into a completely unknown urban milieu, finding a housing shortage, and being forced to set up a squatter house. All the household heads of Kampong Setor were, however, born in rural areas, largely in the states of Selangor, Malacca and Negri Sembilan. Their arrival in Kuala Lumpur has been spread out over some years. Four came before 1950; 7 between 1950 and 1955; 5 between 1955 and 1960, and 7 after 1960. The majority were single when they first arrived in Kuala Lumpur (13 out of the 23) and 5 who were married came first without their families, but had subsequently brought them. Only 5 travelled with their families to Kuala Lumpur. Most have lived elsewhere in Kuala Lumpur, largely in Kampong Bharu where they boarded as single persons. The main reasons they put forward for moving to Kampong Setor was the desire for more spacious accommodation once they were married, and started to have children.

If the picture of the migratory and recent residential patterns of the household heads in squatter kampongs appears to break down the generalized image of the squatter settlement consisting largely of recent migrants in the city, information on the past occupations and present occupations of household heads seems to conform to the general picture of rural migrants moving to the city for economic reasons. Eighteen of the household heads had been occupied in rural occupations prior to moving to Kuala Lumpur, and all of these informants gave their main reason for coming to Kuala Lumpur as their desire to gain a better livelihood. The conditions in the rural area had ceased to be promising. Incomes were dropping, they claimed, and they had been forced out in order to gain a steady income. The occupations of the five other household heads were: police force (three), a teacher and a mechanic. All these people had come to Kuala Lumpur on transfer and were the ones who had brought their families with them, and were still occupied in the same profession. The present occupations of the remainder were very mixed; five were in low-scale office jobs as clerks or office boys; three were drivers; three were watchmen; two were gardeners, and the remainder were engaged in unskilled occupations such as labouring. With the exception of those who had been transferred to Kuala Lumpur, it is clear that all the migrants had entered low-status occupations which only demanded the limited skills they possessed. The fact that police were residing in illegal squatter kampongs is perhaps of some interest, considering the attitude of the city authorities. There were no unemployed in the sample; most evidence pointed towards the fact that if unemployment occurred, the head of the household would send his wife and family back to his home village where they would live until he obtained employment again.

Most of the families in the squatter kampong retained close links with their home village. Many of the men who had come as single men to Kuala Lumpur had attained relatively secure jobs and then gone back to their home villages to arranged marriages with village girls. On returning to Kuala Lumpur with their wives, they moved into squatter areas, largely because of the need for more spacious accommodation. Most of them returned at least once or twice a year to their home village, and many remitted sizeable portions of their income to their parents. The retention of close contacts with their rural home village is common amongst the more recent migrants to the city, although there is a tendency for the number of visits to decline in relation to the length of residence in the city.

The educational backgrounds of the household heads showed almost universal education in Malay up to the top of the primary level. Three household heads, however, had no education, and were illiterate and one household head had an English primary education. Inability to speak English was generally regarded as an extreme limitation to job opportunities in the city. Many of the informants who were asked what language they would prefer their children to be educated in, replied 'English'—primarily because this would give their children greater opportunities for education and better jobs in the future. The majority of the male household heads were deeply religious, attended mosque once a week, and were attached to surau praying groups. Their other activities were largely devoted to films, or listening to the radio. Some grew a few vegetable and fruit crops in their compounds. A common feature united them—the fear of eviction without the provision of adequate housing. To avoid this, they had elected a Ketua Kampong (head of the kampong) who was responsible for contacting the authorities if the city government threatened eviction. The problems of this kampong were remarkably few, even though its levels of income were low; an average of $100 Malayan per month; job stability was high, unemployment low; and in general, the squatter kampong gave every impression of rapid adaption and assimilation to the problems of the urban environment. It could by no means be labelled a 'settlement of misery', but rather a 'settlement of necessity'—a necessity brought about by the lack of adequate city housing.

THE INNER CITY TENEMENTS

The densely packed inner city cores of the Southeast Asian cities forms the area which to the Westerner is most easily recognizable as slums. The Chinatowns have their Western counterparts in Harlem or in the East End of London. They share the common characteristics of physical overcrowding, decaying housing with inadequate amenities, but here the affinities cease.

The inner city cores of the large Southeast Asian cities contain sizeable proportions of the total population. Thus the 378,000 people who occupy the central core of Singapore make up 41 per cent of the population; the 145,000 in the inner area of Rangoon constitute some 20 per cent of the population, and the 485,000 in the core of Manila almost 50 per cent of the total population. The densities in the inner core areas average over 100,000 people per square mile, very much higher than the residential densities of the Western cities. For instance Manhattan, the core of New York city had a density of 80,000 per square mile in 1956.

What are the characteristics of these tenement slums? First in the context of Southeast Asia, they are generally occupied by a population alien to the majority indigenous community of the country. Thus in Rangoon, it is the Indian quarter in which the worst tenement slums occur; in Bangkok it is the Chinese quarter of Samphanthawong; in Singapore, the Chinese quarter stretching from Anson Road to the Singapore River;

in Manila, the Binondo Chinatown and its environs; and in Djakarta a similar pattern is repeated. Thus the description of 'slum' in the Southeast Asian city is typically the description of the Chinatown. Barrington Kaye's account of the Singapore Chinatown virtually applies to every Southeast Asian city:

> Chinatown is a grid of streets consisting almost entirely of two and three storey shop-houses. These shop-houses, originally intended to house one or two families, have been subdivided by a maze of interior partitions into cubicles, the majority of which are without windows and in permanent semi-darkness. Most of these cubicles are about the size of two double beds, placed side by side. In one such cubicle—dark, confined, insanitary, and without comfort—may live a family of seven or more persons. Many of them sleep on the floor, often under the bed. Their possessions are in boxes, placed on shelves to leave the floor free for sleeping. Their food, including the remains of their last meal, is kept in tiny cupboards, which hang from the rafters. Their clothes hang on the walls, or from racks. Those who cannot even afford to rent a cubicle may live in a narrow bunk, often under the stairs.[11]

Another feature of these areas is the fact that work and residence are combined. The shop-house has a dual function of providing residence and a place for commerce. With such densities it is not surprising that the streets are constantly crowded; overcrowding forces the population into the streets to shop, to play, to eat, and to communicate.

In the West, the slum has an emotive connotation. It is an area of crime, of poverty, of danger. The same cannot be said of a Chinatown. It is an area which has produced a distinct pattern of life and distinct patterns of associations, which socially, at least, does not deserve the label of 'slum'. The features of these areas can be illustrated by reference to one area, Upper Nanking Street in Singapore city.

TENEMENT SLUMS—Upper Nanking Street

The characteristics of one tenement slum area have been closely analysed by Barrington Kaye in his survey of Upper

Nanking Street in Singapore. This street is about 220 yards long, consisting almost entirely of two and three storey shop-houses, backing on to shop-houses of streets running parallel to it. In the daytime the street has a great deal of activity: hawkers selling food and people coming out of the shops, to talk, gossip and to buy. The ground floors of most of these shop-houses are devoted to small factories or workshops or to retailing. The second and third floors are partitioned into numerous small cubicles for residents. In 1955 when this survey was carried out, some 1,814 people were resident in Upper Nanking Street. Two features of the demographic structure of the street are of some interest; the high proportion of population in the old-age groups and the preponderance of females in these brackets. The population was divided into some 632 households of which the average size was three persons. The type of household was quite mixed; 39 per cent were single persons; 4 per cent were kongsi;[12] 24 per cent married couples; 11 per cent single parent with children; 13 per cent greater families; [13] and some 10 per cent in other categories.

The physical conditions under which this population lived were extremely cramped. The mean numbers of cubicles and spaces in each shop-house was eight; and the mean shop-house population was thirty. This means that the average cubicle population was 3·3 persons. Over half (56 per cent) of the inhabitants of the street lived in households occupying a single cubicle; 7 per cent were obliged to share a cubicle with another household; and 4 per cent had no other accommodation than the whole or part of the bunk space. There were 103 persons who had only a 'moving space' using a camp bed set up in store-rooms. The average size of the cubicles was 103 square feet. There were ninety-four cubicles with an area of less than 60 square feet and many of the cubicles had no external lighting or ventilation. The inadequacy of living conditions was obvious in the lack of sanitation, toilets and cooking facilities.

Many of these households were made up of Cantonese, and this supports Hodder's[14] assertion about the tendency of Chinese dialect groups to concentrate in a particular part of

Chinatown. One of the most frequent assertions about the character of the population of the Chinatowns, the claim that the majority of the population had been born in China, is not supported in the Nanking Street survey. For the results showed that 59 per cent of the population had either been born in Singapore or the Federation of Malaya. The educational levels of the population were much lower than those of the Malay squatter area; 58 per cent of the population had received no schooling, and the remainder had been largely educated in Chinese-medium primary schools. Of the total resident population surveyed, 42 per cent had some form of full-time employment, and the ratio of employment between men and women was only slightly different—47 per cent of the men and 30 per cent of the women. Most of the women were employed in the rubber factories. The men's jobs were mixed—street vendors, motor fitters, retail shop assistants, hawkers, etc.—but largely jobs which were located within Chinatown. Unemployment was not marked. Despite the problems of the lack of physical amenities and overcrowding, it is incontestably true that the Chinatowns of Southeast Asia do offer a unique way of life and hence do attract a population. Slums they may be, but it seems likely that the cultural and kinship ties of the Chinatown community will continue to attract people.

SLUMS AND SQUATTER SETTLEMENTS—Potential
Danger Spots of the Southeast Asian City

There seems no lack of agreement amongst the planners and civil servants responsible for city government in Southeast Asia that slums and squatter areas are problem areas. The question is, how does the planner set about solving this dilemma. For both areas the same somewhat ambitious answer is given—'resettlement'.

It must be realized that no matter how ambitious resettlement schemes are, they must be regarded as only temporary solutions. Many of the large city governments of Southeast Asia are today facing up to these problems to a varying degree. For instance, the city authorities of Manila, after many years of procrastination, demolished the squatter settlement within the walls of the Intramuros, shifting 11,000 squatters to Sapang Palay, a small municipality, some sixteen miles from Manila city. The process of the shift was extremely badly organized, and the squatters were virtually forced into the new area and left to build their own shacks again. In the area the squatters had left, it was intended to restore the ancient Spanish walls, to repave its streets, and to transform the whole of Intramuros into a cultural centre.

Although they have been more highly organized and provided better housing, similar patterns of squatter resettlement have occurred in Kuala Lumpur, particularly with reference to squatter settlements located near the city's centre. It would appear that national prestige, more than concern for the social welfare of squatters has been the most active force leading to their shift in these two cases. However, there are other examples in Southeast Asia where programmes of squatter resettlement and low-cost housing building programmes have been progressing at a very fast rate. The best example of this is the case of Singapore city. The creation of a Housing and Development Board in 1960 has been responsible for an extremely active programme of low-cost housing building. In 1961 it was estimated that there would be 147,000 housing units needed by 1970, made up of 80,000 units for the resettlement of overcrowded populations from the central areas; 20,000 units needed for people resettled because of central area redevelopment; and 47,000 needed for the natural increase of population. The programme of building development has thus aimed to build something like 15,000 dwelling units per year, of which 10,000 are to be built by the government for lower income groups, and the remaining 5,000 by private enterprise for middle and higher income groups. All the main housing estates have been planned—namely, St. Michael's which will have 3,707 units, with a population of 26,000; Tanjong Rue having 8,000 units with a population of 50,000; Toa Payoh having 30,000 units with a population of 250,000 people; and Queenstown having 17,500 units with a population of 150,000. The minimum size of the unit will be one-room units. The provision of amenities will be much better than those existing in the present shop-house area.[15] Considerable progress in accomplishing this programme has been made but there is still doubt if the building rate can keep pace with the population growth of Singapore City.

CONCLUSION

However, throughout Southeast Asia today the problems of housing the overcrowded populations of the cities are not all being tackled with the energy of the welfare socialism of the Singapore government. In most cities squatter settlements proliferate and slums persist. The population of these areas forms, a potentially dangerous mass of political dynamite for their economic and housing grievances offer a '. . . fertile ground for revolutionary propaganda . . . ,'[16] which could turn the mass of the city populations against their present governments. While the provision of adequate housing may alleviate some of these grievances, at the most it is only a piecemeal measure which does not solve the more basic problems of unemployment and enlarging the economic base of the city. Indeed, such measures may divert valuable finance into housing which might have been spent on industrial development which in the end would be more rewarding for the city population. The slums and squatter areas of the Southeast Asian cities are simply symptoms of a wider condition of economic underdevelopment. The solution lies thus in overall planning rather than the piecemeal engineering of resettlement schemes.

Hauser has pointed out that the countries of Asia have two distinct advantages which aid such schemes of overall planning. First, modern technology '. . . offers a wider range of possibilities for the region-wide distribution of population'.[17] For example, '. . . there is available for industrialization and spatial arrangement of plant and population in Asia electric power as well as steam power, so that cities can simultaneously, rather than sequentially, experience centrifugal and centripetal forces'.[18] Secondly, Asian countries have, 'the advantage of the increasing role of government and public responsibility in the planning of the development process'.[19] With these two advantages the Southeast Asian countries could well take the positive steps needed to guide the process of urbanization.

CHAPTER 10

The Future of the Southeast Asian City

ONE OF the main themes running through this study has been the comparison of the features and growth of Southeast Asian cities with the pattern of urbanization which has emerged in the Western industrialized societies. The value of such an exercise lies not so much in the obvious conclusions that Southeast Asian cities are different, but rather in the fact that it enables the writer to establish the unique elements of Southeast Asian urbanization, and a critical evaluation of the roles of the cities in the process of social and economic development of their countries.

The preceding analysis of city growth points clearly to the fact that the economic, political and social conditions underlying the process are very different from conditions which existed in Western Europe at the time of the first urban explosion. The relentless demographic pressure of rapidly increasing populations associated with the failure of many of the independent governments of the area to accomplish economic development in a period of political instability have turned many of the cities into refuge camps rather than centres of economic development.

While it is clear that the economic conditions in both city and countryside have been important contributory factors in the city growth in Southeast Asia, the major causes are to be found in the political and social conditions of these states in the period since 1947. The process of urbanization in Western Europe was accomplished in states which had largely established national stability and efficiently working national state frameworks.[1] The process of city growth in Southeast Asia is occurring in countries which have not yet established national consensus either in terms of their goals of development or even, in some cases, in terms of the territory they control; nor for that matter have many of them established efficiently working government institutions which would enable the state to proceed with economic and social development. In simple terms, the postwar period in Southeast Asia has been one in which *custodial goals* have been the main concern of governments; not *developmental goals*. The struggle to build efficient and stable nation-states has dominated the energies of the governments to such an extent that the kind of economic and social development which might have been the basis for the growth of new patterns of urban development has not got off the ground. Consequently, the role of the cities has been very different from that which they played during a comparable period of city growth in Western Europe.[2]

The predominance of one great city in the urban hierarchy has persisted in the postwar era, further emphasizing the problems of the relationship between city and countryside. For it means that one city, 'the primate city', in which the urban-based governments are centred, has continued to dominate development in the country. The great city has become the institutional focus, which is represented as being both the peak of the national ethos and the centre from which the new nationalism is disseminated to the outlying regions of the country. The great city is the centre at which a large part of the new nation's political and psychological energies are dissipated; the centre where the country's major industries and services are concentrated; the centre where a large proportion of the country's educated are focused and the major part of the country's wealth. The city presents a paradoxical picture. The needs of nationalism demand that the symbols of the national unity of the pre-colonial past must be utilized, displayed and disseminated to the country's population. Museums and monuments—concrete symbols of the country's historical tradition—proliferate and figure prominently in the new buildings of the Southeast Asian capitals. Yet at the same time, the city must be aggressively modern and Western for the city embodies the concrete hopes of the emergence of a modern industrialized nation.

The cities of Southeast Asia are thus reverting to a

dominantly political role not dissimilar in many ways to that role which the great 'sacred' cities played in the pre-industrial era. This concentration of the nation's active forces in its great city presents many problems for the country, for increasingly the country's conflicts tend to be centred around the manœuvrings of the city-based cliques. Within the city a situation is created—just as in India—where growing numbers of unemployed, 'whom Hoselitz calls the "lumpen proletariat", provide the raw material for the mobs. Political parties, trade unions, business and religious groups, displaced landlords, and princes willing to provide ideological, financial and organizational resources for making effective use of these two groups are not scarce in the cities.'[3] The city mobs can be manipulated by the various groups for their political advantage until the city is brought to the point of anarchy. One need only look at recent events in South Vietnam and Indonesia to see the evidence. At the same time the problems of the countryside prove too intractable for the urban-based governments, and they are ignored or barely touched.[4] It is thought that the adherence of rural support can be bought through the propagation of national slogans. The country's leader, 'the maker of the slogans', begins to assume the charisma and character of the 'god-king' of the pre-industrial city. But increasingly he and his government are isolated from the true feelings of the population of the countryside. Thus the wall that existed between the city and the countryside in the colonial period is reinforced in this new period of nationalism.

It is perhaps inevitable that the city-born governmental *élites* of the new nation should choose to use the city as the chief institutional and organizational means by which nation-state unity is established. The nationalist revolutions and movements through which they achieved the newly acquired independence of their own country were largely urban-based, and it is feasible to suppose, from their point of view, that the process of nation-state unity can be accomplished from a similar urban base. But it is important to remember that the colonial period was characterized by an urban-based power structure of colonial government. The transition to independence was essentially one of urban-based governments being taken over by urban-based nationalist movements. Yet the process of establishing nation-state unity is essentially one of incorporating *all* elements within the country, and the majority of the populations of Southeast Asia are rural. The majority of Southeast Asian governments still have to face the vital question, 'Can the city-based *élites* convince the vast rural populations of these countries of the necessity to adhere to the form and structure of the nation-state which they envisage'?

No simple answer can be given to this question. Basically it rests on the ability of these city-based governments to institute programmes of economic development which will increase the productivity and levels of living in their societies. It seems clear that the type and form of these developments will vary from country to country, as will the relative importance that is given to developments in the rural and urban sectors. In some countries, such as the Philippines, a radical reform of the agrarian structure is necessary if rural production is to be increased. In others such as Thailand, it is necessary to introduce schemes of health and education as well as improved agricultural techniques if the rural population is to increase its incomes. In others it would appear that little can be accomplished until political stability has been achieved. The reality of Southeast Asia is that, with rare exceptions, programmes of economic development have bogged down.[5] The need to divert the energies of the new countries to the task of nation building has prevented these developments and increased the antagonism between city and countryside for as Keyfitz points out,

> When the cities grow as rapidly as they are growing in much of the under-developed world today, and when this growth is accompanied by a relative inertia of industry, then the pressure which the cities have to place on the remainder of their national territory in order to draw their food by taxes, tariffs, exchange control, or other means, is likely to accentuate the element of force in administration.[6]

A situation is thus created in which the city-based governments, failing to bring about economic changes and political adherence in the countryside, increasingly adopt forceful measures and alienate the countryside even more. Diem's repression of the rural opposition to his policies in South Vietnam is a classical example of such a sequence of events. This combination of political oppression and economic stagnation forces the rural migrant into the city, but here the situation is no better. For the city-based governments have failed to reform the economic base of the cities and employment opportunities are lacking—thus rural poverty is replaced by urban poverty.

The contradictions of this vicious circle are further aggravated by the high rates of natural increase in both countryside and city. For a time, perhaps, both areas can absorb these increases in population, the countryside by the intensification of agriculture within the existing agrarian structure, the cities by propping up their economies with foreign aid and food supplies. But eventually, unless some radical economic and social change occurs, an 'explosion' point will be reached. In some cases this explosion may well involve a repetition of the Chinese experience in which a rural-based revolution 'captured' the city-based power structure of the country. In other cases it may well be that growing economic problems force the urban-based governments to adopt the radical changes which they have hitherto largely ignored. Whatever form these developments take, it seems that they must inevitably see some decline in the importance of the great cities of Southeast Asia. The period of great city dominance in Southeast Asia will then be at an end.

NOTES

CHAPTER 1

1. This definition of the boundaries of the Third World accepts the broad delineation of the region put forward by Buchanan (1964) in his article, 'Profiles of the Third World', which includes the communist societies of China, Cuba and North Vietnam. For a dissenting definition see Worsley (1964), *The Third World*, pp. ix–x, and Buchanan (1966).

2. The problem of arriving at some adequate cross-cultural definition of what constitutes an urban area has not been solved. Throughout this study, unless otherwise stated, the urban population is defined as that population resident in 'Urban places' of more than 100,000 population.

3. These figures are estimated from Table 2, 'World Population and World Urban Population, 1800–1960' in the essay by Lampard, 'Historical Aspects of Urbanization', p. 524 in Hauser and Schnore (eds.) (1965), *The Study of Urbanization*, and Table 1, 'World Population by Regions, 1920–60 by Decade', in the United Nations Department of Economic and Social Affairs (1963), *1963 Report on the World Social Situation*, p. 6.

4. See Table 4, 'Share of World's Large City (100,000 and Over) Population by Major Continental Region' in Hauser (ed.), *Urbanization in Asia and the Far East* (1957), p. 58.

5. Urbanized societies represent those countries in which the majority of the population (over 50 per cent) is resident in towns and cities. See Davis (1965), p. 41.

6. See Gottman (1961) for a discussion of the term 'megalopolis'.

7. Davis (1965), pp. 41–53.

8. *Ibid.*, p. 52.

9. See Reissman (1964), *The Urban Process: Cities in Industrial Societies*, pp. 165–6, for an elaboration of this argument.

10. See Wertheim's essay on the 'Urban Characteristics of Indonesia' in *East-West Parallels* (1964), pp. 165–81. Gerald Breese has recently introduced the broader term 'subsistence urbanization' to imply 'urbanization in which the ordinary citizen has only the bare necessities, and sometimes not even those for survival in the urban environment'. Breese (1966), p. 5.

11. Reissman, *op. cit.*, p. 189.

12. See Eisenstedt (1957), pp. 294–5, for an elaboration of this argument. Also Emerson (1955).

13. De Briey (1965), p. 4.

14. Lévi-Strauss (1963), p. 3.

15. See Hoselitz (1960), 'Population Pressure, Industrialization and Social Mobility', pp. 115–37, in his *Sociological Aspects of Economic Growth*.

16. See Hsueh Mu-Chiao, Su Hsing and Lin Tse-Li (1960), *The Socialist Transformation of the National Economy in China*.

17. Two articles give the most comprehensive survey of the general patterns and characteristics of the cities of Southeast Asia: Fryer (1953), 'The "Million City" in Southeast Asia', and Ginsburg (1955), 'The Great City in Southeast Asia'.

18. These estimates are based on Table 7 in the *United Nations Demographic Yearbook, 1960* (1960), pp. 306–25, and Table 3 in Lampard, *op. cit.*, p. 548.

19. Fisher (1964), *Southeast Asia*, p. 187. A critical analysis of the concept of primacy is carried out by Linsky (1965), pp. 506–13 in which an attempt is made to identify the conditions which give rise to primacy. The concept of primate cities was first put forward by Mark Jefferson in 1939. He defined the primate city in a number of ways ranging from the capital to the largest city. But to qualify for the title the capital had to have twice as many people as the next largest city. A glance at Table 1 indicates that all the capitals of Southeast Asia fit this definition.

20. Tinker (1965), 'The City in Asia' in *Reorientations*, p. 46.

21. See Wernstedt and Simkins (1965), pp. 83–103.

22. Stockwin (1965), p. 468.

CHAPTER 2

1. See McGee (1960), pp. 39–41 for a wider discussion of this aspect of early political organization in Southeast Asia.

2. This does not deny the importance of the Chinese influence on urban settlement in the Vietnamese lands, but their influence was nowhere as widespread as that of the Indian systems.

3. Whole books have been devoted to the descriptions of the meaning of the 'deva-raja', but the most succinct analysis that I have read occurs in Coedès (1963) in which he traces the origin of the 'cult of the Devaraja'.

> In the Hinduized kingdoms of Indochina and Indonesia Hinduistic cults especially of Siva accentuated a tendency already apparent in India itself and developed into the cult of royalty. The royal essence, or as referred to in several texts, the 'inner self', was supposed to reside in a *linga* ensconced in a pyramid in the exact centre of the royal city which in turn was located in the centre of the world. This miraculous linga, a kind of palladium of the kingdom, was supposed to have been obtained from Siva through an intermediary who was a Brahmin priest, who then gave it to the first king of the dynasty. This communication between the king and the god through the mediation of a priest took place on the sacred mountain located at the centre of the capital (pp. 29–30).

4. Wheatley (1962), p. 33.

5. See Benda (1965), p. 234.

6. Tinker (1965), p. 31.

7. Coe (1961), p. 83.

8. Spencer (1954), p. 140.

9. See Hall (1955), pp. 25–6.

10. See Wertheim (1956), pp. 168–9. Also Keyfitz (1961), pp. 348–9

11. Spencer, *op. cit.*, p. 140.

12. Tinker (1965), p. 31.

13. Wheatley (1963), p. 179.

14. Foucar (1963), pp. 25–30.

15. Coedès (1963), *op. cit.*, p. 40.

16. *Ibid.*, p. 20.

17. Briggs (1951), p. 219.

18. Coedès (1963), *op. cit.*, p. 96.

19. Coe (1961), *op. cit.*, p. 73, citing Coedès (1947), 'Pour Mieux Comprendre Angkor'. I can find no similar statement in the 1963 translation.

20. Coedès, *op. cit.*, p. 107.

21. The following description is drawn largely from Chapter XX of Wheatley's (1961) pioneer study in the historical geography of the Malayan Peninsula before 1500, 'The golden Khersonese', pp. 306–20.

22. *Ibid.*, p. 312.

CHAPTER 3

1. See van Leur (1955) for an excellent description of the character of Asian trade during this period.

2. See Geertz (1960), *The Religion of Java*, for the role of the coastal cities in the dissemination of the Islamic religion throughout the Malay world.

3. Sternstein (1965(a)) gives a most thorough account of the Western trading posts in Ayutthaya in his article entitled 'Krung Kao: The Old Capital of Ayutthaya'.

4. Zaide (1949), p. 191, citing Laubach, F.C., *The People of the Philippines*, New York (1925), p. 81.

5. See Collis (1946), *The Land of the Great Image* for a beautifully written account of Friar Manrique's travels in Burma.

6. It is interesting to note that India's position as a food deficient state, already apparent in the sixteenth century, persists until the present day.

7. Collis (1946), *op. cit.*, p. 120.

8. Van Leur (1955), p. 137.

9. This description of Malacca is based on the account in Ho (1962).

10. See Kernial (1961), p. 5.

11. Wertheim (1956), p. 170.

12. 'The internal structure of the old Javanese cities, was characterized by a *Kraton* or court in the centre of the city. Near by was an *alun-alun*, a great square on which many communal activities took place and

around which an open or covered market place, houses of nobles, and various other buildings were arranged.' Keyfitz (1961), p. 349.

CHAPTER 4

1. See Wertheim (ed.) (1958), pp. 5–15.

2. Caldwell (1963) gives an excellent account of the growth of the urban network in Malaya in his article, 'Urban Growth in Malaya: Trends and Implications'.

3. Ginsburg (1955), p. 455.

4. Fryer (1953), p. 475.

5. Puthucheary (1960), p. 24.

6. See Burchett (1956), p. 174.

7. Skinner's history of the Chinese in Thailand (1957) gives a most thorough description of the role of the Chinese in the indigenous Thai economy, particularly Chapters 3 and 7. More recently an interesting article by Jackson (1965) reveals the role of the urban-based Singapore Chinese in financing agricultural development in the Malay-controlled state of Johore.

8. Redick (1961), p. 82.

9. See Fryer (1953), *op. cit.*, pp. 490–1.

10. See Skinner (1957), *op. cit.*, Chapter 3, pp. 91–125.

11. See Redick (1961), *op. cit.*, p. 77.

12. See Hoselitz's (1960) article entitled 'Generative and Parasitic Cities', in *Sociological Aspects of Economic Growth*, pp. 185–215.

13. *Ibid.*, p. 191.

14. Motwani (1963), p. 103.

15. Hoselitz (1960), *op. cit.*, p. 192.

16. See Weber (1921), pp. 74–5.

17. Secretariat of the Economic Commission for Asia and the Far East, 'Problems of Industrialization in Relation to Economic Development in the Countries of Asia and the Far East', *Economic Bulletin for Asia and the Far East*, Vol. XI, No. 3, December 1958, p. 5.

18. Abu-Lughod (1965), p. 428.

19. See Jose Rizal's novel, *Noli Me Tangere* for description of this atmosphere.

20. Spate and Trueblood (1942), pp. 56–73. The description of the ecological patterns of Rangoon is based on the excellent series of maps which appear in the Spate and Trueblood article.

21. *Ibid.*, p. 72.

22. See Hodder (1953), for a description of Raffles' original plan of Singapore, pp. 25–6.

23. See Dobby (1940), p. 101.

24. See Donald Davies (1960), *More Old Singapore* for some vignettes of European colonial life in Singapore.

25. See Roff (1964), for a thorough analysis of the Malay community in Singapore at this time.

26. Hodder (1953), *op. cit.*, pp. 25–36.

27. Hall (1955), p. 396.

28. Sommerville (1897), p. 30.

29. Young (1907), p. 19. He also makes the interesting comment that Bangkok was unique amongst the colonial cities at that time because it had no clearly demarcated area for the Europeans. Compare this with the impact of the colonial structure on the residential ecology of Singapore and Rangoon where there were carefully demarcated European areas.

CHAPTER 5

1. Spencer (1958), p. 291.

2. *Ibid.*, p. 289.

3. Chua (1964), *Report on the Census of Population State of Singapore, 1957.*

4. See Louis Wirth's (1938) pioneer paper on the subject, 'Urbanism as a Way of Life', *American Journal of Sociology*, Vol. 44 (July) No. 2, pp. 1–24. Reprinted in Hatt & Reiss (1959), pp. 46–63.

5. See Gourou (1955).

6. For instance, the Federation of Malaya estimate of 42·8 of its total population as urban is almost certainly too high for it includes many 'New Villages' where the employed population is largely engaged in agriculture. The most comprehensive discussion of the problem of defining urban areas in Southeast Asia, with particular emphasis on Indonesia, can be found in Milone (1966).

7. Ginsburg (1955), p. 457.

8. See Wernstedt (1957), pp. 336–46.

9. Smith (1952), p. 60. Milone (1966) indicates that there is 'strong evidence' in Indonesia that there is a lower birth rate in urban areas than rural areas. In addition the urban death rate in Java is appreciably lower than that of the Javanese rural areas. pp. 95–6.

10. See Purcell (1951), *The Chinese in Southeast Asia*, for the most thorough treatment of this topic.

11. H. J. Heeren (1955), p. 699.

12. This is a useful definition for the cities which are growing rapidly from in-migration from rural areas, for it does help to explain why some cities of the Third World have rural characteristics in an urban milieu. The original definition was made by Irene Taeuber in *The Population of Japan*, 1958, p. 150. For an enlarged discussion of the definition see my article, 'The Rural-Urban Continuum Debate: The Pre-industrial City and Rural-Urban Migration', *Pacific Viewpoint*, Vol. V. No. 2, September 1964, pp. 159–81.

13. See McGee (1965a), pp. 207–18, for additional material on the features of rural-urban migration in Southeast Asia.

14. See Buchanan (1965), pp. 366–81.

15. Redick (1961), p. 82.

16. See Heeren (1955), pp. 696–736.

17. Ginsburg (1955), *op. cit.*, p. 457.

18. See Ramos (1961), pp. 89–117, for an enlarged discussion of this aspect.

19. Department of Statistics, Federation of Malaya (1964).

20. *Ibid.*, p. 2.

21. See Wertheim (1964), pp. 173–4.

22. See Skinner (1957), pp. 306–10.

23. See Leifer (1964), pp. 1115–21.

24. These figures are calculated from Table 17, 'Distribution of Families by Income Class by Region: 1961', *Journal of Philippine Statistics*, Vol. XVI, No. 4, 1963, October–December, Department of Commerce and Industry, Bureau of the Census and Statistics, Manila.

25. Lubis (1963), p. 61.

26. The role of the Indonesian intellectual in Djakarta city is discussed in van der Kroef (1954), pp. 133–88. See also pp. 61–93.

27. Bruner (1961), p. 508.

28. Hauser (1957), pp. 87–8.

29. Pye (1962), p. 93.

30. The social characteristics of these 'urban village communities' are indirectly described in a short story by a Burmese novelist writing under the pseudonym of 'N.N.' (1960), 'Stranger in a Kwetthit', *The Orient Review and Literary Digest*, Vol. II, No. 5, Burma Number, pp. 25–48. How little the contemporary city has changed is revealed when this description of Rangoon is compared with an early nineteenth-century account of Jogjakarta by John Crawford. . . . 'The town is divided into a series of quarters, called in the native language campong, a word which, in fact, means a village, and conveys a correct notion of what a Javanese town truly is, not an assemblage of dwellings laid out into streets, lanes and squares, but an aggregate of villages, generally parted from each other by stone walls or bambu fences.' 'Notes on the Population of Java', *The Journal of the Indian Archipelago and Eastern Asia*, Vol. 3, 1849, Singapore, p. 43.

31. See McGee (1965(b)), pp. 7–9.

32. Bruner (1961), *op. cit.*, p. 513.

33. Ramos' article already cited has an extremely full discussion of the problems of city government in the booming metropolis of Manila. In addition reference should be made to Selosoemardjan (1962) for a discussion of the administrative problems in the district of Jogjakarta in Indonesia. Milone (1966) also gives a full discussion of the administrative structure of Indonesian towns.

34. McGee (1963), pp. 178–96.

35. See Murphey (1957) for an extensive discussion of this problem of the creation, or lack of creation of new capitals in Asia, pp. 216–43.

36. Abueva (1963), p. 7.

37. *Newsweek*, January 31, 1966, p. 29.
38. Taylor (1966), p. 21.
39. *Ibid.*, p. 16.
40. Geertz, Hildred (1963), p. 34.
41. Withington (1962), pp. 59–67.
42. See Wernstedt (1957), *op. cit.*, pp. 336–46.
43. Geertz, Hildred (1963), *op. cit.*, p. 39.
44. Freyn (1963), pp. 601 and 605.
45. Hart (1955), p. 31.

CHAPTER 6

1. For instance Caplow has shown that some of the European cities diverge strikingly from the patterns of demographic growth which have been observed in the United States. Theodore Caplow (1952), 'Urban Structure in France', *American Sociological Review*, Vol. 17, No. 5, pp. 544–9. See, also, the excellent discussion in Wilkinson's (1957) unpublished Ph.D. dissertation presented at Colombia University, *Tokyo: A Demographic Study* (1957).

2. Schnore discusses the significant role of transportation in bringing about residential deconcentration in his study of Latin American cities. Schnore (1965), pp. 380–2.

3. Skinner (1957), p. 311.

4. See Weber (1899), pp. 285–300.

5. See Casis, Ana and Davis, Kingsley (1946), 'Urbanization in Latin America: Part II: Traits of the Urban and Rural Population', *Milbank Memorial Fund Quarterly*, Vol. XXIV, No. 3 (July), pp. 34–8.

6. Population Branch, Bureau of Social Affairs, U.N.O., 'Demographic Aspects of Urbanization in the ECAFE Region', in Hauser (ed.) (1957), p. 108.

7. Hunt (1962), 'Changing Sex Ratio in Philippine Cities'. Unpublished paper presented to the I.G.U. Regional Conference on Southeast Asia held at Kuala Lumpur.

8. The most recent statement on this subject occurs in Bureau of Social Affairs, U.N.O., 'Implications of Population Trends for Planning Urban Development and Housing Programmes in ECAFE Countries', in *Economic Commission for Asia and the Far East* (1964), pp. 108–9.

9. Skinner (1957), *op. cit.*, p. 312.

10. Bruner (1963), pp. 1–12.

11. See Djamour (1959).

12. Van der Kroef (1954), pp. 162–9.

CHAPTER 7

1. See Burgess (1925), in Theodorson (ed.) 1961, p. 39. It should be noted that the Burgess zonal hypothesis has been modified substantially by later investigators, notably Homer Hoyt's 'sector theory' and Harris

and Ulman's 'multiple nuclei theory'. However, all these theories assume a relatively homogeneous economic system and are not adequate in explaining the patterns of economic activity which occur within the Southeast Asian city.

2. Geertz, Clifford (1963), *Peddlers and Princes: Social Change and Economic Modernization in Two Indonesia Towns.*

3. *Ibid.*, p. 28.

4. *Ibid.*, p. 30.

5. *Ibid.*, p. 28.

6. I have not included a discussion of the market-gardening zone which surrounds all these large cities. The characteristics of the Singapore market-gardening zone have been described by Blaut (1953) and Ho (1964).

7. Rowley (1960), p. 33.

8. These figures are taken from a cyclostyled copy of the 1959 Census of Phnom-Penh.

9. McIntyre (1955), pp. 66–80.

10. See Iain Buchanan's observations on the social role of Western shopping centres in Singapore. 'Singapore', *N.Z. Listener*, June 11, 1965, pp. 5 and 21.

11. Redick (1961), pp. 89–97.

12. See Murphey (1957), Fisher (1964), Ginsburg (1955), and Fryer (1953), for a discussion of the features of the ports of Southeast Asia.

13. 'Report on the Economic Aspects of Malaysia', *Mission of the International Bank for Reconstruction and Development,* Government Printing Office, Singapore, 1963.

14. This trade has completely stopped since Indonesian confrontation began in 1963.

15. See State of Singapore (1960), '*Report on the Commission of Inquiry into the System of Contract Labour in Singapore*'.

CHAPTER 8

1. These studies are too numerous to list here. But amongst them, Louis Wirth's *The Ghetto*, stands out as a classic sociological study of one of the many communities which existed in Chicago at this time.

2. See Burgess (1925), pp. 37–44.

3. See Sjoberg (1960), pp. 97–9.

4. This data was taken from the Philippines Census, 1960. It is one of the few primary sources for Southeast Asia which provides detailed information on the ownership of such assets as radios, and the type and standard of housing. See also Hunt's description of the ecological areas of Manila in Chapter 15 'The Urban Community', in *Sociology in the Philippine Setting* (1963), pp. 284–303.

5. Dwyer (1964) reports that these squatters have been finally shifted out of the Intramuros area.

6. See my article on 'The Cultural Role of Cities: A Case Study of Kuala Lumpur', for an enlarged discussion of the residential patterns of Kuala Lumpur. Also see Bennett (1961), pp. 237–333.

7. This description is taken from McGee and McTaggart (1967), *Petaling Jaya: A Socio-Economic Survey of a New Town in Selangor, Malaysia.*

8. See in particular, U.N.O., 'Public Administration Problems in the New and Rapidly Growing Towns of Asia' (1962), and Watts (1953), pp. 19–26.

CHAPTER 9

1. See McGee (1961), pp. 101–5.

2. See Abrams (1964), pp. 13–14.

3. *Ibid.* (1964), Chapters One and Two, pp. 1–24.

4. This information on the number of squatters is taken from Dwyer (1964) and Abrams (1964).

5. Dwyer (1964), pp. 146 and 151.

6. See Teulierès (1962), pp. 166–79.

7. See Abrams (1964), p. 16.

8. See van der Kroef (1954), p. 172.

9. Lubis (1963), p. 18.

10. See McGee (1965(b)), pp. 7–9.

11. Kaye (1960), p. 2.

12. Kongsi: Kaye (1960) defines the term as follows:

    '(i) a group of single persons living together and sharing household expenses, or (ii) the dormitory of the house they use', p. 7.

13. A greater family consists of three generations of relatives, in-laws, and/or married siblings. Kaye (1960), p. 32.

14. See Hodder (1953), pp. 25–36.

15. See Housing and Development Board Singapore, 1961, *Annual Report.*

16. Abrams (1964), p. 287.

17. Hauser (1957), p. 29.

18. *Ibid.*, p. 90.

19. *Ibid.*, p. 29.

CHAPTER 10

1. This is not to deny the fact that the cities of western Europe played an important role in the process of nation building. As Murphey (1954) has pointed out:

    'The city has instigated or led most of the great changes in Western society, and has been the centre of its violent and non-violent revolutions. In Western Europe, the city has been the base of an independent entrepreneur group which has successfully challenged and broken the authority of the traditional order,' p. 330.

2. Rhoads Murphey has discussed these comparative aspects of the role of the cities in two different socio-economic systems in his article entitled, 'The City as a Center of Change. Western Europe and China' (1954). See also Redfield and Singer (1954), Hoselitz (1960), McGee (1963).

3. Tangri (1962), p. 199. Note the two groups he refers to also include the 'lumpen intelligentsia'—the unemployed educated who appear to be of importance in only two areas of Southeast Asia—Indonesia and South Vietnam.

4. It must be admitted, however, that some Southeast Asian countries have been making efforts to improve the standards of living and increase production in rural areas. North Vietnam, faced with perhaps the most difficult rural situation because of the very great densities of its rural population, has adopted radical measures of agricultural reform. In Malaya, where the ruling political party draws most of its support from the dominantly rural Malays, there has also been an emphasis on rural development, with measures aimed largely at increasing rural production and amenities rather than radical changes in the agrarian structure.

5. This does not deny that there has been some industrial development in the Southeast Asian countries. Rather it emphasizes that the quantity of this industrial development has not been adequate to cope with the problems of economic take-off.

6. Keyfitz (1965), p. 265.

BIBLIOGRAPHY

A. BASIC STATISTICAL SOURCES

This list of statistical sources consists only of those sources from which I have taken information incorporated in this study. Many of the publications of the various statistical organizations of the Southeast Asian governments and United Nations are published regularly and offer an invaluable continuing source on Southeast Asian cities and countries.

☆   ☆   ☆

Biro Pusat Statistik, 1962, 'Sensus Penduduk, 1961, Republik Indonesia' (Population Census, 1961. Republic of Indonesia) Kabinet Menteri Pertama, Djakarta.

— 1963, 'Sensus Penduduk 1961, Selurun Indonesia. Angka-Angka Sementara' (Population Census, 1961. Whole of Indonesia. Preliminary Figures). Serie: S.P. 1 Kabinet Menteri Pertama, Djakarta.

Central Statistical Office, National Economic Development Board, Thailand, 1961, 'Thailand Population Census, 1960, Changwad Series, Changwad Phranakhorn; Changwad Thonburi', Bangkok.

— 1962, 'Thailand Population Census, 1960, Whole Kingdom', Bangkok.

Chua, S. C., 1960, 'State of Singapore. Report on the Census of Population 1957', Singapore.

Del Tufo, M. V., 1949, 'Malaya comprising the Federation of Malaya and the Colony of Singapore. A Report on the 1947 Census of Population', Kuala Lumpur and Singapore.

Department of Commerce and Industry, 1962, 'Census of the Philippines: 1960. Population and Housing, Vol. I, Report by Province, Manila; Rizal', Bureau of the Census and Statistics, Republic of the Philippines, Manila.

— 1963, 'Census of the Philippines: 1960. Population and Housing, Summary Report', Bureau of the Census and Statistics, Republic of the Philippines, Manila.

— 1963, 'Journal of Philippines Statistics', Vol. XVI, No. 4, October and December, Bureau of the Census and Statistics, Republic of the Philippines, Manila.

Department of Statistics, Federation of Malaya 1958, 'Household Budget Survey of the Federation of Malaya, 1957–58', Kuala Lumpur.

— 1964, 'Report on Employment, Unemployment and Under-employment, Federation of Malaya, 1962', Kuala Lumpur.

Fell, H., 1960, '1957 Population Census of the Federation of Malaya', Department of Statistics, Kuala Lumpur.

Housing and Development Board, Singapore, 1961, *Annual Report, 1961*, Singapore.

International Urban Research, 1959, 'The World's Metropolitan Areas', Berkeley and Los Angeles, University of California Press.

Ministère du Planification, Royame du Cambodge, 1959, 'Recensement de la Population au Cambodge, Phnom Penh'. Unpublished, cyclostyled.

U.N.O., 1958, 'Economic Development and Planning in Asia and the Far East. Industrialization'. Economic Bulletin for Asia and the Far East, Vol. IX, No. 3, December, New York.

U.N.O., Department of Economic and Social Affairs, 1959, 'The Population of Asia and the Far East, 1950–1980. Population Studies, No. 31', New York.

— 1960, 'Demographic Yearbook, 1960', New York.

— 1962, 'Public Administration Problems in the New and Rapidly Growing Towns of Asia', New York.

— 1963, '1963 Report on the World Social Situation', New York.

— 1964, Economic Commission for Asia and the Far East, 1964, 'Report on the Asian Population Conference and Selected Papers', New York, 1964.

— 1965, 'Economic Survey of Asia and the Far East, 1964', Economic Bulletin for Asia and the Far East, Bangkok.

B. BOOKS AND ARTICLES

The following list of books and articles represents only a small fragment of the literature concerning the Southeast Asian city. I have indicated with an asterisk those books and articles which are most important in building up a comprehensive picture of Southeast Asian urbanization.

☆　　☆　　☆

*Abrams, Charles, 1964, Man's Struggle for Shelter in an Urbanizing World, Cambridge, Mass.

Abueva, Jose, V., 1963, 'Social Backgrounds and Recruitment of Legislators and Administrators in a Developing Country: The Philippines'. Unpublished paper presented to the UNESCO, East–West Major Project Symposium on 'Leadership and Authority', pp. 1–22.

Abu-Lughod, Janet, 1965, 'Tale of Two Cities: The Origins of Modern Cairo', Comparative Studies in Society and History, Vol. VII, pp. 429–57.

*Azambre, G., 1955, 'Hanoi: notes de géographie urbaine', Bulletin Société. Etudes Indochinoises, Saigon, T. XXX, No. 4, pp. 355–63.

Benda, Harry J., 1965, 'Political Élites in Colonial Southeast Asia, An Historical Analysis', Comparative Studies in Society and History, Vol. VII, April, pp. 233–51.

Bennett, W. J., 1961, 'Kuala Lumpur: A Town of the Equatorial Lowlands', Tijdschrift voor Economische en Sociale Geografie, Vol. 52, No. 12, pp. 327–33.

Blaut, J. M., 1953, 'The Economic Geography of a One-Acre Farm on

Singapore Island', The Malayan Journal of Tropical Geography, Vol. I, October, pp. 37–48.

Boeke, J. H., *Economics and Economic Policy of Dual Societies*, New York, 1953.

Breese, Gerald, 1966, *Urbanization in Newly Developing Countries*, Inglewood Cliffs, New Jersey.

*Briggs, Lawrence Palmer, 1951, 'The Ancient Khmer Empire', Transactions of the American Philosophical Society, New Series, Vol. 41, Part I, Philadelphia.

Broek, J. O. M., 1957, 'The Ports of Borneo', Technical Report No. 1. Department of Geography, University of Minnesota, Minneapolis. (Mimeo.)

*Bruner, Edward M., 1961, 'Urbanization and Ethnic Identity in North Sumatra', American Anthropologist, Vol. 63, No. 3, June, pp. 508–21.

Bruner, Edward M., 1963, 'Medan: The Role of Kinship in an Indonesian City', in Spoehr, Alexander (ed.) *Pacific Port Towns and Cities. A Symposium*, Bishop Museum Press, 1963, pp. 1–12.

Buchanan, Keith, 1964, 'Profiles of the Third World', Pacific Viewpoint, Vol. 5, No. 2, September, pp. 97–126.

Buchanan, Keith, 1965, 'Cambodia, Oasis of Peace', The Geographical Magazine, Vol. XXXVIII, No. 5, September, pp. 366–81.

Buchanan, Keith, 1966, 'The Third World—and beyond', Outlook, Vol. 10, No. 1, pp. 7–9.

Buckley, C. B., 1902, *An Anecdotal History of Old Times in Singapore*, Singapore, 2 vols.

Burchett, Wilfred, 1956, *North of the Seventeenth Parallel*, Delhi.

Burgess, Ernest W., 1925, 'The Growth of the City: An Introduction to a Research Project', in Theodorson, George A. (ed.) 'Studies in Human Ecology', 1961, Elmsford, New York, pp. 37–44. Reprinted from 'The City', 1925 (ed.) Park, Robert E., Burgess, Ernest W., McKenzie, R. D., Chicago, pp. 47–62.

Cady, John F., 1964, *Southeast Asia: Its Historical Development*, New York.

Caldwell, J. C., 1963, 'Urban Growth in Malaya: Trends and Implications', Population Review, January, pp. 39–50.

*Carelli, G., 1961, 'A Saigon l'Oriente si fonde con l'Occidente', Vie Mondo, 1961, T. XXIII, No. 3, pp. 253–65.

Chabot, H. T., 1964, 'Urbanization Problems in Southeast Asia', Transactions of the Fifth World Congress of Sociology, Vol. III, Louvain, Belgium, pp. 125–31.

Chesneaux, Jean, 1949 and 1950, 'Notes sur l'évolution récente de l'habitat urbaineen Asie', L'Information Géographique, Vol. 13, 1949, pp. 169–75 and Vol. 14, 1950, pp. 1–8.

Coe, Michael D., 1961, 'Social Typology and Tropical Forest Civilizations', Comparative Studies in Society and History, Vol. IV, No. 1, Nov., pp. 65–85.

*Coedès, Georges, 1963, *Angkor. An Introduction* (trans. Gardiner, Emily Floyd), London.

*Collis, Maurice, 1946, *The Land of the Great Image*, London.

*Cressey, Paul, 1950, 'Rangoon. A Brief Social Survey. Rangoon Gazette Ltd., Rangoon.

Cressey, Paul, 1956. 'The Ecological Organization of Rangoon, Burma', Sociology and Social Research, Vol. XI, January, pp. 166-9.

Davies, Donald, 1956, *More Old Singapore*, Singapore.

Davis, Kingsley, 1965, 'The Urbanization of the Human Population', Scientific American, September, Vol. 213, No. 3, pp. 41-53.

De Briey, Pierre, 1965, 'Urbanization and Under-Development', Civilisations, Vol. XV, No. 4, Bruxelles, pp. 2-14.

De Briey, Pierre, 1966, 'Urban agglomerations and the modernisation of the developing states', Civilisations, Vol. XVI, No. 1, Bruxelles, pp. 3-25.

Djamour, Judith, 1959, *Malay Kinship and Marriage in Singapore*, London.

Dobby, E. H. G., 1940, 'Singapore: Town and Country', The Geographical Review, Vol. XXX, No. 1, January, pp. 84-109.

*Dwyer, D. J., 1964, 'The Problem of In-Migration and Squatter Settlement in Asian Cities: Two Case Studies, Manila and Victoria-Kowloon', Asian Studies, Vol. II, No. 2, pp. 145-69.

Eisenstadt, S. N., 1957, 'Sociological Aspects of Political Development in Underdeveloped Countries', Economic Development and Cultural Change, Vol. V, No. 3, April pp. 289-307.

Emerson, R., 1955, *Representative Government in Southeast Asia*, Cambridge, Mass.

Fisher, Charles A., 1964, *South-East Asia. A Social, Economic and Political Geography*, London.

Foucar, E. C. V., 1963, *Mandalay the Golden*, Dobson, London.

Fraser, J. M., 1952, 'Town Planning and Housing in Singapore', Town Planning Review, April, No. 23, pp. 5-25.

Freedman, Maurice, 1957, *Chinese Family and Marriage in Singapore*, Colonial Office: Colonial Research Studies, No. 20, London.

Freyn, Hubert, 1963, 'Profile of Nakorn Sritamaraj', Far Eastern Economic Review, August 29, Hong Kong, Vol. XLI, No. 9, pp. 601-5.

*Fryer, D. W., 1953, 'The Million City in Southeast Asia', Geographical Review, October, pp. 474-94.

Furnivall, John S., *Netherlands India: A Study of Plural Economy*, Cambridge (Eng.), 1944.

Geertz, Clifford, 1960, *The Religion of Java*, London.

*Geertz, Clifford, 1962, 'Social Change and Economic Modernization in Two Indonesian Towns: A Case in Point', in Hagen, Everett E., 'On the Theory of Social Change', Homewood, Illinois, The Dorsey Press.

Geertz, Clifford, 1963, *Peddlers and Princes. Social Change and Economic Modernization in Two Indonesian Towns*, Chicago.

Geertz, Hildred, 1963, 'Indonesian Cultures and Communities', in McVey, Ruth T. (ed.) 'Indonesia', Southeast Asia Studies, Yale University and H.R.A.F. Press, pp. 24-96.

George, Pierre, 1962, 'Matériaux et Réflexions pour une Politique urbaine rationnelle dans les Pays en Cours de Développement', Tiers Monde, Vol. III, pp. 337–59.

*Ginsburg, N. S., 1955, 'The Great City in Southeast Asia', American Journal of Sociology, March, Vol. 60, No. 5, pp. 455–62.

Ginsburg, N. S., 1965, 'Urban Geography and the Non-Western Areas', in Hauser, Philip M., and Schnore, Leo F. (eds.), The Study of Urbanization, New York 1965, pp. 311–46.

Goh Keng Swee, 1958, 'Urban Incomes and Housing. A Report on the Social Survey of Singapore, 1953–54', Singapore, 1958.

Gottman, Jean, 1961, Megalopolis: The Urbanised Northeastern Seaboard of the United States, New York.

Gourou, Pierre, 1955, The Peasants of the Tonkin Delta: A Study in Human Geography, Human Relations Area Files Press, New Haven, Conn., 1955.

Groslier, B. P., 1954, 'Une enquête démographique et sociale sur un quartier de Saigon-Cholon', Bulletin Société Etudes Indochinoises, Saigon, T. XXIX, No. 1, pp. 4–17.

*Groslier, B. P., 1958, Angkor et le Cambodge au XVI siècle d'après les sources portugaises et espagnoles, Paris.

Hall, D. G. E., 1955, A History of Southeast Asia, London.

Hall, Peter, 1966, The World Cities, London.

Hamzah, Sendut, 1962, 'Patterns of Urbanization in Malaya', The Journal of Tropical Geography, Vol. 16, October, pp. 114–30.

Hamzah, Sendut, 1964, 'Urbanization', in Wang Gungwu (ed.), Malaysia, A Survey, New York, pp. 82–96.

Hart, Donn V., 1955, The Philippine Plaza Complex: A Focal Point in Culture Change, Cultural Report Series No. 3, Yale University, Southeast Asia Studies.

*Hauser, Philip M. (ed.), 1957, Urbanization in Asia and the Far East, Tensions and Technology Series, UNESCO, Calcutta.

Hauser, Philip M., and Schnore, Leo F. (eds.), 1965, The Study of Urbanization, New York.

Heeren, H. J., 1955, 'The Urbanization of Djakarta', Ekonomi dan Keuangan Indonesia, November, Vol. 8, No. 11, pp. 696–736.

Heine-Geldern, Robert, 1942, 'Conceptions of State and Kingship in Southeast Asia', Far Eastern Quarterly, Vol. II, November, pp. 15–30.

Ho, Robert, 1962, 'Guide to Tours' (Kuala Lumpur, Regional Conference of Southeast Asian Geographers).

Ho, Robert, 1964. 'Mixed-Farming and multiple-cropping in Malaya', The Journal of Tropical Geography, Vol. 16, pp. 1–17.

Hodder, B. W., 1953, 'Racial Groupings in Singapore', The Malayan Journal of Tropical Geography, Vol. I, October, pp. 25–36.

*Hoselitz, Bert F., 1960, Sociological Aspects of Economic Growth, Glencoe, Illinois.

BIBLIOGRAPHY

Hoselitz, Bert F., 1962, 'The Role of Urbanization in Economic Development: Some International Comparisons', in Turner, Roy (ed.), *India's Urban Future*, Berkeley and Los Angeles, pp. 157–81.

Hsueh Mu-Chiao, Su Hsing and Lin Tse-Li, 1960, *The Socialist Transformation of the National Economy in China*, Foreign Languages Press, Peking.

Huberman Leo and Sweezy, Paul, M., 1965, 'War and Revolution', Monthly Review, Vol. 17, No. 6, November, pp. 1–11.

Hunt, Chester L., 1962, 'Changing Sex Ratio in Philippine Cities', Unpublished paper presented to the I.G.U. Regional Conference on Southeast Asia held at Kuala Lumpur.

Hunt, Chester L., 1963, *Sociology in the Philippine Setting*, Quezon.

Indo-China, 1943, Geographical Handbook Series, Naval Intelligence Division, B.R. 510.

Jackson, James C., 1965, 'Chinese Agricultural Pioneering in Singapore and Johore, 1800–1917', Journal of the Malaysian Branch, Royal Asiatic Society, Vol. XXXVIII, Pt. I, 1965, pp. 77–105.

Kaye, Barrington, 1960, Upper Nankin Street Singapore. A Sociological Study of Chinese Households Living in a Densely Populated Area, Singapore.

Kernial Singh Sandhu, 1961, 'Chinese Colonization of Malacca: A Study in Population Change 1500–1957 A.D.', The Journal of Tropical Geography, Vol. 15, June, pp. 1–26.

Keyfitz, Nathan, 1961, 'The Ecology of Indonesian Cities', American Journal of Sociology, Vol. 66, No. 4, pp. 348–54.

*Keyfitz, Nathan, 1965, 'Political-Economic Aspects of Urbanization in Southeast Asia', in Hauser, Philip M. and Schnore, Leo F. (eds.), *The Study of Urbanization*, pp. 265–309.

Koop, John Clement, 1960, 'The Eurasian Population in Burma', Cultural Report Series No. 6. Yale University Southeast Asia Studies, New Haven.

*Kroef, J. M. van der, 1954 and 1956, *Indonesia in the Modern World*, Part I, Masa Baru, Bandung, Part II, Masa Baru, Bandung, 1956. In particular Chapter 4 of Part I, 'The City: its Culture and Evolution', pp. 133–88.

Lampard, Eric E., 1965, 'Historical Aspects of Urbanization', in Hauser, Philip M. and Schnore, Leo F. (eds.), *Study of Urbanization*, pp. 519–54.

Lee, Y. L., 1962, 'The Port Towns of British Borneo', Australian Geographer, Vol. 8, No. 4, pp. 161–73.

Leifer, Michael, 1964, 'Communal Violence in Singapore', Asian Survey, Vol. IV, No. 10, October, pp. 1115–21.

*Leur, J. C. van, 1955, *Indonesian Trade and Society*, The Hague.

Lévi-Strauss, Claude, 1962, 'Crowds', New Left Review, No. 15, May–June, pp. 3–6.

Lewis, John P., 1964, *Quiet Crisis in India Economic Development and American Policy*, Anchor Books, Doubleday and Co., Inc., Garden City, New York.

Lewis, W. Arthur, 1955, *The Theory of Economic Growth*, London.

Lim Tay Boh, 1960, *The Development of Singapore's Economy*, Background to Malaya Series, Eastern Universities Press, Singapore.

Lin Piao, 1965, 'Long Live the Victory of the People's War', Peking Review, September 3, pp. 9–30.

Linsky, Arnold, S., 1965, 'Some Generalizations Concerning Primate Cities', Annals of the Association of American Geographers, Vol. 55, No. 3, September, 1965, pp. 506–13.

MacMillian, Allister, 1926, *Seaports of the Far East*, W. H. and L. Collingridge, London.

McGee, T. G., 1960, 'Aspects of the Political Geography of Southeast Asia, A Study of Period of Nation-Building', Pacific Viewpoint, Vol. I, No. 1. March, pp. 39–58.

McGee, T. G., 1961, 'The Asian City: Problems and Prospects', Pacific Viewpoint, Vol. 2, No. 1, March, pp. 101–5.

McGee, T. G., 1963, 'The Cultural Role of Cities: A Case Study of Kuala Lumpur', The Journal of Tropical Geography, Vol. 17, May, pp. 178–96.

McGee, T. G., 1964, 'The Rural-Urban Continuum Debate: The Pre-Industrial City and Rural-Urban Migration', Pacific Viewpoint, Vol. 5, No. 2, September, pp. 159–81.

*McGee, T. G., 1965(a), 'An Aspect of Urbanization in Southeast Asia: The Process of Cityward Migration', Proceedings Fourth N.Z. Geography Conference, Dunedin, pp. 207–18.

McGee, T. G., 1965(b), 'An Aspect of the Urban Geography of Malaysia. The Movement of Malays to Kuala Lumpur City', New Zealand Geographical Society Record, January–June, No. 39, pp. 7–9.

*McGee, T. G. and McTaggart, W. D., 1967, Petaling Jaya. A Socio-Economic Survey of a New Town in Selangor, Malaysia. Pacific Viewpoint Monograph, No. 2.

*McIntyre, W. E., 1955, 'The Retail Pattern of Manila', Geographical Review, January, Vol. 45, No. 1, pp. 66–80.

McVey, Ruth T. (ed.), 1963, *Indonesia*, Southeast Asia Studies, Yale University and H.R.A.F. Press, New Haven.

Milone, Pauline D., 1964, 'Contemporary Urbanization in Indonesia', Asian Survey, Vol. IV, No. 8, August, pp. 1000–12.

Milone, Pauline, Dublin, 1966, *Urban Areas in Indonesia; Administrative and Census Concepts*, Research Series No. 10, Institute of International Studies, University of California, Berkeley.

Motwani, X., 1963, 'The Impact of Modern Technology on the Social Structures of South Asia', in UNESCO, 'Social Change and Economic Development', pp. 99–109.

*Murphey, Rhoads, 1954, 'The City as a Center of Change: Western Europe and China', Annals of the Association of American Geographers, Vol. XLIV, pp. 349–62.

*Murphey, Rhoads, 1957, 'New Capitals of Asia', Economic Development and Cultural Change, Vol. V, No. 3, April, pp. 216–43.

Murphy, Raymond E. and Vance, J. E. Jnr., 1959, 'Delimiting the C.B.D.', in Mayer, Harold M. and Kohn, Clyde, F., *Readings in Urban Geography*, pp. 418–46. Originally published in Economic Geography, Vol. XXX, July 1954, pp. 189–222.

Neville, R. J. W., 1962, 'An Urban Study of Pontian Kechil, South-West Malaya', The Journal of Tropical Geography, Vol. 16, October, pp. 32–56.

*Neville, R. J. W., 1963, 'Singapore; Recent Trends in the Sex and Age Composition of a Cosmopolitan Community', Population Studies, Vol. 17, pp. 99–112.

Neville, R. J. W., 1965, 'The Areal Distribution of Population in Singapore', The Journal of Tropical Geography, Vol. 20, June, pp. 16–25.

No Author, 1900, European Settlements in the Far East, London.

Pal, Agaton P., 1963, 'Dumaguete City, Central Philippines', in Spoehr, Alexander (ed.), Pacific Port Towns and Cities, pp. 13–16.

Palmier, Leslie H., 1958, 'Western Communities in Southeast Asia', Yale Review, Vol. 47, pp. 405–15.

Palmier, Leslie H., 1960, Social Status and Power in Java, London.

Puthucheary, J. J., 1960, Ownership and Control in the Malayan Economy, Eastern Universities Press, Singapore.

Pye, Lucien W., 1962, Politics, Personality and Nation Building, Burma's Search for Identity, New Haven, Massachusetts Institute of Technology, Centre for International Study.

Rama Rau, Santha, 1958, View to the Southeast, London.

*Ramos, Carlos P., 1961, 'Manila's Metropolitan Problem', Philippine Journal of Public Administration, Vol. 5, No. 2, April, pp. 89–117.

*Redfield, R. and Singer, M. B., 1954, 'The Cultural Role of Cities', Economic Development and Cultural Change, Vol. 3, No. 1, October, pp. 53–73.

*Redick, Richard W., 1961, 'A Demographic and Ecological Study of Rangoon, Burma'. Unpublished Ph.D. thesis, University of Chicago.

*Redick, Richard W., 1964, 'A Demographic and Ecological Study of Rangoon, Burma, 1953', in Burgess, Ernest W. and Bogue, Donald J., Contributions to Urban Sociology, Chicago, 1964, pp. 31–41.

Reissman, Leonard, 1964, The Urban Process. Cities in Industrial Societies, Glencoe, Illinois.

Roff, W. R., 1964, 'The Malayo-Muslim World of Singapore at the Close of the Nineteenth Century', Journal of Asian Studies, Vol. XXIV, No. 1, November, pp. 75–90.

Rowley, C. D., 1960, The Lotus and the Dynamo: A Traveller in Changing Southeast Asia, Angus and Robertson Ltd., Sydney. Particularly Chapter 4, 'Asian City', pp. 31–49.

Santos, Milton, 1961, 'Quelques problèmes des grandes villes dans les pays sous-développés', Revue de Géographie de Lyon, No. 3.

Schnore, Leo F., 1965, 'On the Spatial Structure of Cities in the Two Americas', in Hauser, Philip M. and Schnore, Leo F. (eds.), The Study of Urbanization, New York, pp. 347–98.

Seck, Assane, 1965, 'Introduction à l'étude des villes tropicales', Tiers Monde, Vol. VI, pp. 171–204.

Selosoemardjan, 1962, Social Changes in Jogjakarta, Ithaca, New York.

*Sjoberg, Gideon, 1960, *The Preindustrial City, Past and Present*, Glencoe, Illinois.

*Skinner, G. William, 1957, *Chinese Society in Thailand: An Analytical History*, Ithaca, New York.

Smith, T. E., 1952, *Population Growth in Malaya*, London.

Sommerville, Maxwell, 1897, *Siam on the Meinam*, London, Sampson Low, Marston and Co.

*Spate, O. H. K. and Trueblood, L., 1942, 'Rangoon: A Study in Urban Geography', Geographical Review, January, Vol. 32, pp. 56–73.

Spencer, J. E., 1951, 'Changing Asiatic Cities', Geographical Review, April, Vol. 41, pp. 336–7.

Spencer, J. E., 1954, *Land and People in the Philippines*, Berkeley and Los Angeles.

Spencer, J. E., 1954, *Asia East by South: A Cultural Geography*, New York.

*Spencer, J. E., 1958, 'Cities of the Philippines', Journal of Geography, September, pp. 288–94.

*Sternstein, Larry, 1965(a), ' "Krung Kao": The Old Capital of Ayutthaya', The Journal of the Siam Society, Bangkok, Vol. LIII, January, 1965, pp. 84–121.

*Sternstein, Larry, 1965(b), 'A Critique of Thai Population Data', Pacific Viewpoint, Vol. 6, No. 1, May 1965, pp. 15–38.

Stockwin, Harvey, 1965, 'Complacency in Kuala Lumpur', Far Eastern Economic Review, Vol. L, December 29, pp. 464–8.

Stokes, Charles J., 1962, 'A Theory of Slums', Land Economics, August, pp. 187–197.

Suyin, Han, 1961, 'Kuala Lumpur: Roofs Among the Jungle Trees', Life, Vol. 30, No. 6, March 27, pp. 46–57.

Tan-Kim Huon, 1961, *Géographie du Cambodge*, Phnom Penh.

*Tangri, Shantri, 1962, 'Urbanization, Political Stability and Economic Growth', in Turner, Roy (ed.), *India's Urban Future*, Berkeley and Los Angeles, pp. 192–212.

Taylor, Charles, 1966, 'Bullets and Bargirls', Far Eastern Economic Review, Vol. LI, No. 1, pp. 15–16 and 21.

Teulieres, Roger and Huy, Nguyen, 1962, 'Une Agglomération de Sampans habités à Saigon', Cahiers d'Outre Mer, April–June, pp. 166–79.

Textor, Robert B., 1961, 'From Peasant to Pedicab Driver', Cultural Report Series No. 9, Yale University, Southeast Asia Studies, New Haven.

Theodorson, George A., 1961 (ed.), *Studies in Human Ecology*, Elmsford, New York.

Thompson, P. A., 1906, *Lotus Land: Being an account of the Country and People of Southern Siam*, T. Werner Laurie, London.

Thrupp, Sylvia L., 1961, 'The Creativity of Cities', Comparative Studies in Society and History, Vol. IV, I, November, pp. 53–64.

*Tinker, Hugh, 1965, *Reorientations: Studies on Asia in Transition*, Pall Mall Press, London. Particularly Chapter 2, *The City in Asia*, pp. 29–48.

Uhrenbacher, Werner, 1960, 'Mandalay, Städt der birmanischen Könige und der Pagoden', Kosmos, No. 12, pp. 537–43.

Ullman, Edward L., 1960, 'Trade Centers of the Philippines', Geographical Review, Vol. 50, No. 2, April, New York, pp. 203–18.

Watts, K., 1953, 'Small Town Development in the Asian Tropics', Town Planning Review, No. 1, pp. 19–26.

Weber, Adna Ferrin, 1899, The Growth of Cities in the Nineteenth Century, Ithaca, New York, 1899, reprinted 1963.

Weber, Max, 1921, The City, translated and edited by Martindale, Don, and Neuwirth, Gertrude, Collier Books, New York. Published 1962.

Wernstedt, Frederick L., 1957, 'Cebu: Focus of Philippine Interisland Trade', Economic Geography, Vol. 32, pp. 336–46.

Wernstedt, Frederick L. and Simpkins, Paul D., 1965, 'Migrations and Settlement of Mindanao', The Journal of Asian Studies, Vol. XXV, No. 1, November, pp. 83–103.

Wertheim, W. F., 1956, Indonesian Society in Transition, W. van Hoeve Ltd., The Hague, Bandung.

*Wertheim, W. F. (ed.), 1958, The Indonesian Town, The Hague.

*Wertheim, W. F., 1964, East–West Parallels: Sociological Approaches to Modern Asia, W. van Hoeve Ltd., The Hague, and Bandung. Particularly Chapter 8, 'Urban Characteristics in Indonesia', pp. 165–81.

Wheatley, P., 1954, 'Land Use in the Vicinity of Singapore in the Eighteen Thirties', The Journal of Tropical Geography, Vol. 2, pp. 63–6.

*Wheatley, Paul, 1961, The Golden Khersonese: Studies in the Historical Geography of the Malay Peninsula before A.D. 1500, University of Malaya Press, 1961, Kuala Lumpur.

Wheatley, Paul, 1962, Notes on the Historical Geography of the Malayan Peninsula (mainly before 1900).

Wheatley, Paul, 1963, 'What the Greatness of the City is said to be', Pacific Viewpoint, Vol. 4, No. 2, September, pp. 163–88.

Wikkramatelike, R., 1965, 'Focus on Singapore', The Journal of Tropical Geography, Vol. 20, June, pp. 73–83.

Wilkinson, T. O., 1957, 'Tokyo: A Demographic Study'. Unpublished Ph.D. thesis, Columbia University.

Willmott, Donald Earl, 1960, The Chinese of Semarang: A Changing Minority Community in Indonesia, Cornell University Press, Ithaca, New York.

*Wilson, J. L. J., 1956 (ed.), 'The Asian City', Current Affairs Bulletin, Vol. 19, No. 5, December 24, Department of Tutorial Classes in the University of Sydney.

Wirth, Louis, 1938, 'Urbanism as a Way of Life', The American Journal of Sociology, Vol. XLIV, No. 1, July, pp. 1–24. Reprinted in Hatt, Paul K. and Reiss, Albert J. Jr. (eds.), 1929, Cities and Society, Glencoe, Illinois, pp. 46–63.

Withington, William A., 1961, 'Upland Resorts and Tourism in Indonesia: Some Recent Trends', Geographical Review, Vol. 51, No. 3, July, 1961, pp. 418–23.

Withington, William A., 1962, 'Medan: Primary Regional Metropolis of Sumatra', Journal of Geography, 61, pp. 59–67.

Withington, William A., 1962, 'The Cities of Sumatra', Tijdschrift voor Economische en Sociale Geografie, Vol. 53, pp. 242–6.

*Withington, William A., 1963, 'The Kotapradja or King Cities of Indonesia', Pacific Viewpoint, Vol. 4, No. 1, March, pp. 75–86.

Worsley, Peter, 1964, The Third World, London, 1964.

Young, Ernest, 1907, The Kingdom of the Yellow Robe, London.

Zaide, Gregorio F., 1949, 'Philippine Political and Cultural History, Vol. I, The Philippines Since Pre-Spanish Times', Manila.

Zinkin, Maurice, 1951, Asia and the West, London.

C. NOVELS AND SHORT STORIES

It is not surprising, in view of the dominance of the great Southeast Asian City as a centre of intellectual activity, that much of the contemporary indigenous literature portrays the problems of their changing societies within the milieu of the city. At the same time the great cities have also been the gateway through which the foreign writers enter the countries of Southeast Asia and consequently the large cities have been portrayed by some of the most perceptive of Western observers.

☆　☆　☆

Ambler, Eric, 1956, The Night Comers, Heinemann. A novel set in an imaginary Southeast Asian state which portrays some of the frenzied political activity of the city.

Ambler, Eric, 1959, A Passage of Arms, Knopf. A novel with a Malayan setting.

Boulle, Pierre, 1959, Sacrilege in Malaya (trans. Xan Fielding), Secker and Warburg.

Burgess, Anthony, 1964, Malayan Trilogy, Pan Books. This collection includes, Time for a Tiger, The Enemy in the Blanket and Beds in the East. Set in the postwar Malaya at the time when Independence is near, these novels portray the tragi-comic situation of the multi-racial society of Malaya with bitter humour.

Echols, John M. (ed.), Indonesian Writing in Translation, Ithaca Cornell Modern Indonesia Project.

Echols, John M. (ed.) (1956), Perspective of Indonesia, Atlantic Monthly Supplement. Includes translations of stories by Pramudya Ananta Tur, Armijn Pane, Mochtar Lubis, Asrul Sani, Idrus, and Achdiat Karta Mihardja.

Enright, D. J., 1960, Insufficient Poppy, Chatto and Windus. An amusing tale set in Bangkok city.

Fauconier, Henri, 1931, The Soul of Malaya (trans. Eric Sutton), Matthews and Marriot. A superb picture of the colonial society in Malaya: set in Selangor State, it is concerned largely with the life of planters, but there is one superb description of Kuala Lumpur city and the social life of the Europeans.

Gonzalez, N. V. M., 1960, *The Bamboo Dancers*, The Benipayo Press. While much of this book deals with the life of the Filipino expatriate living in another country, portions of it reveal the life of Manila and the English educated in a most enlightening way.

Greene, C., 1955, *The Quiet American*, Heinemann. Political intrigue in the unreal atmosphere of Saigon city.

Hougron, J., 1958, *Reap the Whirlwind*, Hutchinson, London. The claustrophobic existence of the French community in a small colonial town in Laos.

Kaye, Tom, 1961, *David from where he was Lying*, Abelard. Some excellent descriptions of Singapore's overcrowded Chinatown.

Lubis, Mochtar, 1963, *Twilight in Djakarta* (trans. Claire Holt). Probably the best of the novels and short stories because it portrays the whole spectrum of post-Independence Djakarta society and attempts to show how they relate to one another.

Maugham, Somerset W., 1951, *The Complete Short Stories*, Vol. III. Particularly *Footprints in the Jungle*—(Malacca), *Mirage*—(Haiphong), *The Letter*—(Singapore), William Heinemann, London.

'N.N.', 1960, *Stranger in a Kwetthit*, The Orient Review and Literary Digest, Vol. II, No. 5, Burma Number, pp. 25–48. A short story written by a prominent Burmese writer who uses the pseudonym 'N.N.' This is first-rate account of life in one of the burgeoning squatter colonies of Rangoon.

Ong, Johnny, 1964, *Sugar and Salt*, Times Press and Anthony Gibbs.

Orwell, George (first published 1934), 1955, *Burmese Days*, Secker and Warburg, London. While the setting is not one of the great cities of Southeast Asia this novel portrays the intrigue and life of a European community in a small provincial town in Upper Burma.

Osaragi, Jiro, 1955, *Homecoming*, Knopf. Part of this novel is set in Malaya at the time of the Japanese invasion and accurately records the condition of the towns at this time.

Polotan, Kerima, 1962, *The Hand of the Enemy*, Regal Publishing Company, Manila. Traces the making of one of the 'elegant young Westernized men' of the city of Manila, and the tragedy of the traditional world he discards.

Reynolds, Jack, 1956, *A Woman of Bangkok*, Secker and Warburg. Sophisticated society in Bangkok.

Rizal, Jose, 1961, *Noli Me Tangere* (trans. Leon M. Guerrero). The classic novel of Southeast Asian indigenous literature which attacks the iniquities of Spanish rule in the Philippines in the nineteenth century.

Santos, Bienvenido, 1960, *Brother, My Brother*. A collection of Stories, Benipayo Publishers, Manila.

Suyin Han, 1956, . . . *And The Rain My Drink*, Jonathan Cape Ltd.

West, Maurice, 1965, *The Ambassador*, Morrow. The setting is Saigon-Cholon. The time, the end of the Diem régime. A superb picture of the death throes of a city-based government increasingly isolated from its rural population.

BIBLIOGRAPHY

Wigmore, L. (ed.), *Span: An Adventure in Asian and Australian Writing*, Melbourne, F. W. Cheshire, 1958. Collection of short stories by a variety of Southeast Asian writers.

Wignesan, T., 1964, *Bunga Emas*. An Anthology of Contemporary Malaysian Literature, Anthony Blond with Rayirath (Raybooks) Publications, Malaysia.

Index